Connections:

Linking Life
to Learning

**by K-12 Teachers in the
Rutherford County, Tennessee
School System**

Wax Family Printing, LLC
Murfreesboro, TN

ISBN 0-9726392-7-6 Paperback

Title: Connections, Linking Life to Learning, multiple authors.
Subject: Literary Collections, Poetry.

Project Sponsor:
Rutherford County Tennessee Board of Education
Harry Gill, Jr., Director of Schools

Project Coordinators:
Sheila Bratton, Middle Level Coordinator
Elizabeth Church, Language Arts Instructional Specialist
Jackie Drake, Administrative Assistant

For Wax Family Printing:
Publisher: Kevin Wax
Editor: Kevin Wax
Cover Design and Inside Layout: Angel Pardue

To publish a book for your school or non-profit organization that complements
your academic goals or values, vision and mission, please contact:

Wax Family Printing, LLC
215 MTCS Drive
Murfreesboro, TN 37129

phone: 615-893-4290
fax: 615-893-4295
www.waxfamilyprinting.com

Table of Contents

Chapter One
Connecting through Life's Treasures

Chapter Two
Connecting through Personal Thoughts

Chapter Three
Connecting through Fond Memories

Chapter Four
Connecting through Family Memories

November 9, 2004

Dear Reader,

Once again this summer, Rutherford County teachers participated in the Writers' Academy where they received professional training in the writing process. They have moved from novice writers to published authors, and they will use this training to improve writing instruction in their classrooms throughout the year.

Connections is the fifth in a series of books published to showcase the writings of Rutherford County teachers. Their writings will stir many emotions as you read their sometimes humorous, sometimes sad, but always thoughtful poems, stories, and letters. Please enjoy this collection and make your own connections to the memories and fond remembrances in your own lives.

Best regards,

Harry Gill, Jr.
Director of Schools

Moving Beyond Excellence

Chapter One

Connecting through Life's Treasures

Summer Visions

Heather Stewart
Buchanan Elementary School, Grade 1

Students gone on summer breezes
Like dandelion fluff twirling on air
Spinning fibers from a community of diversity
Tying strings, connecting teachers and parents
Twining cords among educational colleagues
Weaving ropes anchored to community
Creating educational hammocks to cradle children
Facilitating a safety net of support
Mending the cracks, so that falls become flights
Visionary thoughts as I sway back and forth
During a summer-long nap.

Heather Stewart

I is for In-service

Valerie Lay
LaVergne High School, Grade 10

Today's the day, first day of school.
A life-long learner, ain't that cool?
Rush out the door. I can't be late.
We start our class promptly at eight.

Will I be there on time today?
I know the answer—There is no way!
Summer is here. I sleep 'til ten.
But still I'm eager to connect again.

Authors speak and teach and share.
Diligent notes I take with care.
I come alive to write and think.
I hope I use up all my ink!

So much to learn, absorb, apply.
Pass the tissue, I'm gonna cry!
Free books and pens and white out, too.
Teachers scream, "Hooray!" "Yoo hoo!"
        (This is sad, but it is true.)

Teachers as students, we must create.
Suddenly, my thoughts evaporate.
But I must try. I must compose.
My solace is next week's repose.

Random Ponderings of a Teacher

Kim Cing
Siegel High School, Grades 9 and 10

Will they trust me?
Students hide their true selves behind a façade of toughness.
Do they understand just how much I invest daily in their lives, or do they think this is just
        a Job to me?
Can they even guess the sacrifices I make . . . family time, leisure time, rest time?
Am I wrong to assume that they know I care for them almost like my own children?
Would they balk or get discouraged if I challenge them, or would they walk boldly into
        the waiting embrace of learning?
Do they respect me enough to tell me if they disagree with my words or actions?
Will they ever come back to thank me or will they look back and wish they had been in a
        different class?
What will they remember about me? That I was "cool?" That I have a short temper?
        That I was the only one who would listen?
Will they just forget about me?
Have I praised them enough?
Have I criticized too much?
Do they realize that I pray for them?
Would they care?
Did I teach them anything?

Soccer Cycle
Kerri Clark
Rockvale Elementary School, Grade 5

Player
Fast, Nimble,
Playing, Scoring, Winning,
Athlete, Protégé, Mentor, Friend, ·
Planning, Training, Caring,
Wise, Strong,
Coach.

Mother Nature
Latasha Allison
Blackman Elementary School, Grade 3

Mother
Serene, nurturing, gentle, kind
Who loves Earth Day
Who hates mini malls
Who fears bulldozers
Who feels neglected
Resident of the blue-green planet
Nature

A THOUGHT
Camille Gray
Central Middle School, Grade 7

Life is full
Life is small
Life is bright
Life is tall
Life is joy
Life is pain
Life is enjoying ice cream in the rain.

To Whom It May Concern

Monte Parks
Rock Springs Elementary School, Grade 5

To Whom It May Concern:

Why do people drive in the passing lane when they are not passing?

How do words work through the human language? Where do they begin? How does something that Person A says on his front porch in Georgia make it all the way to Person Z's kitchen in California?

Why do the most ignorant and obnoxious people have the most to say?

Why does road construction take so long? It seems that it is never completely finished. Does someone study the busiest times of the day and plan to start working then? Isn't it more dangerous for the road crews to work at this time?

Why does it seem that it takes longer to get somewhere than it takes to get back?

Why does most meat other than beef, pork and fish taste like chicken?
Why do many restaurants and places of business place handicapped parking on the sides of the buildings instead of the front? It seems that causes more trouble for people who must use the spaces. They have to struggle to the front door and I just pop out and make a straight shot in the front door. While I'm on the subject, why do people park in handicapped spaces when they don't need them. That makes me very angry.

Why do I find it so difficult to actually put pen to paper and record my inner thoughts and feelings? Why is it so gut wrenching to admit my true feelings? I know that they are mine and I am entitled to them.

Why can't I make decisions without such agony? I can step back and see that in the grand scheme of things it does not matter, yet I can't just throw caution to the wind.

Why do I have time to sit and ponder about things like this?

If you have the answers to my questions, please write soon. Thank you for your time.

Sincerely,
Me

LIFE?

Jennie Griffin
Rockvale Elementary School, Grades 7 and 8

LIFE is: Living.

Finding your inner PEACE

And

Wondering what will happen next.

LIFE is: Facing your personal fears.

Realizing that, even you make mistakes

And

Loving.

LIFE is: Enjoying what God has given you.

Being the best you can be, both personally and

professionally

And finally-

LIFE is what **you** make of it—so live yours to the fullest!!!

I'm Not There Yet

Richard Reed
Rock Springs Middle School, Grade 8

It's like sitting in the back on the family's yellow Bonneville anticipating
arrival. I'm so anxious to get there.
"Are we there yet?"
"No!"

It's like digging through the cooler in the back seat looking for another
sandwich to eat and occupy time. It's just something to do.
"Are we there yet?"
"No!"

It's like hours of aimless games we play. They take my mind off of the reality of
these mediocre moments, but they really don't accomplish anything.
"Are we there yet?"
"No!"

It's like lying to myself at the sight of every mile marker, telling myself that this
futile journey is almost over. It's a lie, but it keeps me going.
"Are we there yet?"
"No!"

It's like fooling myself into believing that I know where I'm going even though
I truly have no idea. I'm at the mercy of the man in the driver's seat.
"Are we there yet?"
"No!"

It's like- NO...It is LIFE.
Full of billboards that read:
"Life is a journey not a destination."
I hate those!
I'm ready to get somewhere. I want to arrive, but I really don't know what that
means.
"I'm not there yet."

My Angel in Disguise

Ynetia Avant
Lascassas Elementary School, Grade 2

Every child has a teacher that they'll never forget. For me that was my fifth grade teacher. My fifth grade year was one of many changes. My fifteen-year-old sister became pregnant and I was immediately labeled to be next. I also lived with my grandmother because my parents worked nights. So, I entered my fifth grade year with a negative attitude.

I was a very popular student, but on the inside I felt alone. I thought that no one understood my troubles because they didn't have troubles of their own. One day we were at recess and the teachers were sitting under their tree. My teacher called me over and asked me how things were going. I felt like the queen of fifth grade because my teacher was interested in me. I proceeded to tell her all of my bottled up feelings that I had told no one. She then asked me what I wanted out of life. Mrs. Jackson was thrilled when I told her that I wanted to teach. We then began having weekly talks under the "teacher tree." She walked me through the steps I needed to take to get where I wanted to be. High school, scholarships, and colleges were things I knew nothing about, but she told me anyway. Since I was the fastest runner in fifth grade, I set my goal to be a track star and become a T.S.U. Tigerbelle like Wilma Rudolph.

My fifth grade year ended quickly and I had to leave my favorite teacher. I never saw her much after that. However, when I did see her she'd always say, "How's my little Tigerbelle?" What I wanted to tell her was that middle school was so different than elementary. The competition was tough and a Tigerbelle I probably wouldn't be.

When I entered high school being like Wilma Rudolph was definitely out of the question. My grades were not the best. I loved to work and play basketball all the time. My senior year of high school came and I was afraid to go to college. I had taken all the right classes, but I still wasn't sure. At the beginning of the school year, I decided after I graduated I'd take a year off and work to earn money. When basketball season came, we had a new freshman on our team. She immediately came to me and informed me of how much she admired me and wanted to work as hard as she knew I had. The sweet girl then told me that her mother just loved me and talked about me all the time. This young girl was my fifth grade teacher's daughter. I was so impressed and excited; I then had an image to uphold. I graduated in June and headed to Tennessee State University.

Even though I was not a Tigerbelle, I was on the path to becoming a teacher. On May 8, 1999, I earned my degree in education. I walked across the stage and shook the president's hand. As I headed down the steps I saw all of my loved ones lined up to congratulate me. First I saw my mother, then my father, and at the end of that line stood my fifth grade teacher. She grabbed me and held me very tight. As we embraced and sobbed she whispered in my ear, "You did it little Tigerbelle." I knew at that moment she had been with me all the way.

My Angel in Disguise.

Melts in your Mouth

Ava Broadbent
LaVergne Primary School, Grade 1

The chocolate
Savory, soft, yet heavenly
Like an aphrodisiac
It gave my mind a sense of peace
And all my stress dissolved
Like the chocolate in my mouth
The last thought
That I encountered
As it finally disappeared in my mouth
When can I have another?

Rosemary

Karen Elise Burrell
Walter Hill Elementary School, Grade 3

Gathering her sixteen years of strength, my daughter broke the news. "Rosemary died today," she disclosed reluctantly. My stomach became a cement mixer. Plopping into the nearest chair in disbelief, I vacantly stared at our Christmas tree.

How could this be? Not Rosemary! Her resilience through the years had made her an Energizer Bunny. Straight, brown, chin-length hair framed her sun-roasted round face that almost always sported a smile. More than a hint of her Polish Italian heritage was confirmed in her facial features. Every time she opened her mouth she revealed a robust Philadelphia via New Jersey brogue. No, this long time survivor of crisis couldn't be dead!

How many years had it been since our time as college freshmen when we had pledged the same sorority? How often through the years had our lives been woven into common fabric? How long had it been since I had called or written just to touch my friend with words of encouragement? Guilt was an adult elephant lying on my chest. In my busy life, I had neglected this precious person. The distance between Tennessee and Florida was no excuse. Calls and cards should have been more frequent. Urgency had again robbed me of what was more important in life. No chance for a final "good-bye." Even attending the memorial service would be impossible.

Over the next two days I reflected on the many ways Rose's life had intersected with mine during our college years: nights sitting cross-legged on our dorm beds sorting out our love lives; formal dances, giggle sessions, skits, psychology classes, and other special times with our sorority sisters; Rosemary spiritedly directing our All-Sing Choral Group with her foot tapping as only a percussionist's foot could; introducing my United Methodist faith to her world of Catholic icons, saints, and doctrine; exposing my sheltered southern values to seemingly foreign traditions and thoughts from the North; challenging me as a shy, "manner-bound" teenager to speak more boldly and with passion. Candid, yet tactful, or just plain outspoken….Rose spoke her thoughts.

Rosemary shared her darkest teenage incident that had left her afraid of physical intimacy and motherhood. Physical challenges shadowed her. Seizures interrupted her life with exhausting effects. Life threatening allergies to orange juice and seafood made meal choices complex. Rose shared her father's death, her mother's struggles as a single mother of three, and life with her stepfather. Through it all, Rosemary's chuckle erupted spontaneously into full laughter. Positive remained her words and attitude to life.

In college we experienced the tragic death of a friend that was crushed by an oncoming car while on a nighttime bike ride, and the suicide attempt of the girl who had been riding with the victim.

In our twenties, Rose attended my protestant punch and cake wedding. The next year, my husband and I flew to "Philly" for her full banquet, wine, and rock band marriage celebration. Dale, the love of her life, was a Southern "WASP" (White, Anglo-Saxon Protestant) as my husband and I were. Imagine the Steel Magnolia wedding blending with The Godfather! Music ranging from the" "Hokey Pokey" to "Speak Softly Love" nestled between toasts to the bride and groom. Glasses tinkled from silverware blows that signaled the new couple to find each other and kiss.

The wedding guests request for Rose to accompany the band on the drums had to be made only once. Was she ready! Rosemary raised her skirts discreetly and gingerly adjusted her elegant wedding train before breaking loose on a wild rendition of "Wipeout."

As young married couples, we visited with each other at the various places we lived. They came to our trailer within the fence of the National Guard Armory in Knoxville. Our friends experienced a taste of the old south in Millen, and Savannah, Georgia. When I was pregnant with our first child, we moved to Chattanooga where Dale and Rose lived several years before following their dreams to Florida. We picnicked, camped, and spent New Years Eves together. We reveled in our friendships. Even our son's first swim was in their apartment pool.

Rose loved to entertain. Anytime Rosemary prepared a meal, extraordinary care was taken. Presentation of the precisely sliced cheeses and pepperoni was crucial. Real Italian pasta and authentic Polish ingredients were a necessity. Choosing a gift was an art form. Rose searched for *the* perfect Mickey Mouse postcard, *the* exact glass, or *the* most appropriate tee shirt slogan. With each selection, she stroked and caressed each item repeatedly as if adding her affection by the extra touch.

When we reached our thirties, we began to lose contact with Rose and Dale. Careers and time pressures pushed our friendships into the background. However, when I was in the last trimester of my second pregnancy, we flew to Florida for a visit to Mickey Mouse and our long-time friends. It was hard to tell who had the best time in the Magic Kingdom, our son or Rosemary who could be comfortable wearing Mouse Ears in places other adults would cringe.

In our forties we experienced much change. My marriage died and was buried after twenty-one years and two terrific children. Phone calls and affirmations from Rose helped give me added support. Soon change came to our friends as well. Rose and Dale seemed to have evaporated! My attempts to locate them were futile. Eight years had elapsed when I read in a college newsletter that Rose and Dale were celebrating a special anniversary. A phone number was listed. I was thrilled! After resuming our contact, I discovered that they had been forced to remain undercover for an extended time because of Dale's job as an insurance investigator for the state.

After reconnecting, I learned that Rosemary had struggled much of that time with several bouts of cancer. Surgeries, chemotherapy, and battling to get the disability money to which she was entitled consumed much of their time. Whether confined to a wheel chair or walking with assistance, she continued to attend her water aerobics class. Rose was determined to keep her spirits, and the spirits of others, as high as possible.

When Dale said that they had a trip planned to visit family in Tennessee for New Year's, my 15-year-old daughter and I reserved some of the precious time with them. Laughter abounded. Good memories were revisited. Rosemary's prognosis was upbeat. Her future again looked promising. During the next eleven months, however, Rosemary's health was a roller coaster. Amazing comebacks followed drastic problems. Then several days before Christmas, the word that she had passed into eternal life came.

Not able to go to the memorial service, I decided to spend that specific hour at home offering prayers of gratitude for the extraordinary gift of knowing Rosemary. I regretted not sending more words of encouragement or making more calls to cheer.

While questioning whether or not she understood my love for her and admiring her courage in the face of adversities, the doorbell rang. The mailman had left a box wrapped in brown paper addressed to me. Mailed after her death, I knew she had chosen this as a loving connection from her to me. The card was signed in familiar handwriting, "Love, Rose." Tearfully, I unwrapped the package that revealed a rag doll dressed in soft blue and white cotton. I hugged it and cried bittersweet tears. They were tears of joy, forgiveness, and parting. Rosemary *had* understood. I knew just what to do with my new rag doll. I stroked and caressed it repeatedly, as if receiving all of her affection that she had added by her touch.

Chocolate Hips

Tracy Linnell
Stewartsboro Elementary School, Grade 5

The chocolate was sticky
but melted quickly.

It soon got slick
and tasted thick.

It made my mouth water
and my hips larger.

Sailors

Cary Eugene Holman
Homer Pittard Campus School, Grade 5

The journey began some ten months ago
You should have been there to see the show.

With assignments, projects, and field trips in view
Yet little time to spend, before the year would be through.

All too quaint without a faint, sailors began to see
Just what this captain and his ideas would come to be.

First to D.C. and, oh yes, the camp fire then came
We played, danced, and slept, but then some started to complain.

Just yesterday the treasure box displayed it all
The sail of this ship without a doubt was an absolute ball.

From face to face and letter to letter
My fifth grade sailors brought joy, peace, laughter
and made my life better.

Belated Thanks

Melissa Griley
Smyrna High School, Grade 12

I remember you, Mrs. Williams,
Hair always unkempt,
Your mismatched clothes unknowingly accessorized
With chalk stains on the most embarrassing places.

I remember you, Mrs. Williams,
Bravely standing in front of the class,
Determined to teach, unfazed and undeterred
By the glazed expressions on our adolescent faces.

I remember you, Mrs. Williams,
Kind and generous with your time,
And the safe haven you created during lunch
For a scared and confused teenage girl.

I remember you, Mrs. Williams,
And I am ashamed I never thanked you,
Since you were the only teacher that never gave up
Or decided I was beyond reach.

I remember you, Mrs. Williams,
Even though you think I don't,
And your memory is alive in me as I now stand bravely
In front of the classroom determined to teach.

Falling Stars

Corey Brewer
Oakland High School, Special Education, Grades 9-12

If I thought I could have helped you I would have
I feel that I failed in some way
As a teacher I feel that I should have
It's a feeling I still feel today.

The decisions you've made come to haunt me
A life wasted is all that I see
Could one person have helped you to change things
If I'd tried harder could that one have been me.

I would like to think that I taught you
A little of right and of wrong
Through the music you wrote in my classroom
I could already hear your great song.

Your talent was so overwhelming
I think that you could have gone far
It certainly would not have surprised me
If one day you'd been a great star.

But now you sit in a jail cell
A life you chose to take
I can't help but sit and wonder
What difference could I really make.

Your story has made me determined
To not let another star fall
If I help just one student I've succeeded
I just wish that I could help save them all.

Asking for Forgiveness

Joyce Hugle
Wilson Elementary School, Grade 3

As I look back at a student I had a few years ago, I have some regrets. His life has now gone astray.

I wonder what could I have "said" or "done" to prevent this from happening. Was I indifferent to his needs at this time in his life?

What could or should I have done or didn't do? Could I have had more parental contact? Could I have gone to a minister or pastor when I heard he was getting in trouble in upper grades? Could I have stopped him for choosing the wrong path?

Please forgive me for not intervening when one of my students needed me.

Immigrant Girl

Johnna Underwood Torok
Rock Springs Middle School, Grade 6

She holds her new pencil tight,
Clasped in her hand with hope and fear,
Words surround her, words she can't understand,
Filling her soul with noise.

She holds her new country tight
Clasped in her heart with hope and fear,
Opportunities surround her, chances she's never known,
Filling her soul with dreams.

She holds her new teacher tight,
Clasped in her arms with hope and fear,
Teacher's love surrounds her, helping her understand,
Filling her soul with peace.

April Epiphany

Barbara Teichman
Smyrna High School, Grade 11

The moment that I truly knew that I wanted to be a teacher came in the fall of 1973. I was enrolled in the Teacher's College of the University of Cincinnati, and, until then, I think that I was just adopting the dreams of people whom I admired and held dear. That fall I participated in a program called "September Experience," where first year education students spent a month in the field as teacher's aides for part of each day. We were not given a choice of placement, nor were we placed according to our content areas or even our certification goals. We were merely thrust "out there," to see for ourselves what education was all about.

The University of Cincinnati is surrounded by the diversity of a typical urban residential environment. A collage of cultural settings, from privileged to impoverished, was evident within a few blocks of any building on the campus. As an eighteen-year-old freshman, I was alternately stimulated, astonished, or intimidated by the multitude of scenes I encountered everyday.

I am a product of the suburbs. My only contact with an urban environment up till then was a sheltered, chaperoned look at the city through the windows of a school bus or the eyes of watchful adults who whisked me back to the suburbs when I had absorbed all of the urban culture they were comfortable with.

My placement with this program was in a second grade, inner city classroom at Vine Street Elementary School. My supervising teacher's name was Mrs. Anderson, and she was African-American. As a child, I was taught that all prejudice was wrong—but I was surrounded by only one culture. Every student and teacher in my elementary school was white, all of my friends were white and in my high school of over 700 students, only six were black, and one of these was a foreign exchange student from Uganda. In fact, the only African-Americans that I ever came in contact with on a regular basis were non-professional service providers; janitors, cooks, housekeepers, gardeners and general laborers.

I remember getting lost trying to find the school. Unfamiliar with driving on city streets and painfully conscious of the fact that I was driving my mother's car, I couldn't help taking notice of the neighborhood where the school was located. I saw no white people on the corners, around the storefronts, or at the bus stops. Even the few police officers I saw were black. As I desperately tried to recover my bearings so that I wouldn't be late for my first day, it didn't occur to me that people might think my presence in this area was strange. Because of this I was not shocked at orientation, not even surprised when I heard from the principal, who was also African-American, that 98% of the student body was black, and that, including me, the faculty and staff now had three white members; one teacher, one cafeteria worker, and a student teacher aide. I just assumed that things in this school were similar to the schools that I had attended; the population of the school reflected the community around it. After taking a long look at me, and asking if I had any questions, the principal showed me to Mrs. Anderson's second grade classroom.

Mrs. Anderson was a stern, somewhat imperious older woman who seemed to have a permanent frown etched in the corners of her mouth and across her forehead. After the principal retreated to his office, she took stock of me with a disapproving stare and gave me her classroom guidelines. "I run an orderly classroom. These kids come from a world where there are no rules, but plenty of consequences. I don't care if they're afraid of me, I just want to make sure that they know why!" With this, she abruptly turned her back to me, handed me a stack of worksheet pages and told me to start grading.

All that morning, the room was wrapped in almost total silence, except for the drone of the reading group doing their recitations and oral readings in the corner with Mrs. Anderson. While I worked diligently through the stack of papers, I occasionally stole glances at the students and I caught them doing the same at me, but for that entire morning I was never able to talk to the students, nor were they able to talk to me.

As the days passed, Mrs. Anderson began to see the advantage of having me around and used the opportunity of my presence more and more, often disappearing from the classroom for as much as an hour at a time, though not before assigning a considerable amount of work to be completed by morning's end. In those days I had long, straight hair in the "Cher" style popular in the '70's, that hung to the middle of my back. To keep it out of the way in the classroom, and to look more "professional" I attempted to pull it into a tight bun, but inevitably, as I worked my way around the classroom helping first one child and then the next, the hair worked loose and took on a frazzled, unkempt appearance. I finally gave up and wore it in a long ponytail to keep it out of my face.

Something curious began to happen at that point. Perhaps it was the fact that the students began to be more comfortable with me or the fact that Mrs. Anderson wasn't present as often, but as I stooped to help students or knelt by their desks, their natural curiosity took over and I found them staring intensely at my eyes, touching my face and arms, and most of all, stroking my hair.

One little girl in particular touched me more than the others. April was the smallest in the class; a child with warm chocolate brown skin and fawn-like eyes surrounded by long delicate eyelashes. She explored everything around her with a sort of quiet deliberateness; as if she knew she was only going to have a short time to study all of the wonderful things that surrounded her. She listened almost in rapture when I read a story to the group and she delighted in looking through the cigar box full of crayon stubs at the beginning of class, not going for a "favorite," but picking a new color every day. Textures and colors were important to her; she loved to touch my sweaters, feel the scarf I often wore around my neck, and most of all, to stroke my hair. Not a day went by that she didn't timidly raise her hand to ask for help and answer my questions in a soft whisper while she unconsciously stroked the hair of my ponytail.

One morning during my last week with the class, April didn't come to school. The day was cold, gray and blustery, especially so for late September. I thought of April because I was wearing the scarf she liked so much and I realized that I missed her curiosity. When I took the children out to the playground for recess, I noticed Mrs. Anderson talking to the principal and a lady wearing a Children's Services identification badge. Many of the children were curious in a distant, but wary sort of way. "That's the lady that takes kids away," I overheard one of the children say. "I hope my Gran'ma didn' call her!" The other adults motioned for me to come over, and I felt uneasy as I approached them. Mrs. Anderson asked me. "You been spendin' a lot of time with April. 'She say anything to you about things happening at home?" Truthfully, April never said much at all to me. Our communication was on more of a comfortable, unspoken level than that.

"No. Why?" I asked.

"Her mother was found by a neighbor last night, badly beaten, and April was nowhere to be found. The police are searching the neighborhood and areas where her mother's boyfriend hangs out, but so far, no luck. Let us know if you hear anything the kids might say."

I was shocked and devastated, but more so by the casual attitude of the adults in charge of the situation. Mrs. Anderson never mentioned April after that, even when the word came to us three days later that April's body had been found in an abandoned shed behind the garage where the mother's boyfriend worked. The frown merely deepened on the teacher's forehead and her eyes took on a tired, worn-out look as she gathered April's belongings and put them into the lost and found box in the closet.

Two days later the program ended and during that time, not one child asked where she was or what had happened.

Mrs. Anderson met with me on the last day to give me my evaluation and, uncharacteristically, to thank me for my help. I asked her why the children didn't ask questions about April or what happened to her. It wasn't a secret, and had been in the newspapers and on the television since her disappearance.

"You're from the suburbs or you would probably know this, but kids here don't make strong attachments. Nothing's permanent here, except the knowledge that every day you wake up is one more day than yesterday and things that you never take into your heart can't hurt when they're ripped away. Your leaving is going to hurt them most of all, because you're the only white person that most of them have seen up close and you've been nice. That dream will stay with them until reality crowds it out. I hope they don't come to hate you for it." I was struck by an epiphany brought on by her words; she spoke for herself, her students, and her community.

I walked away from that school and those children with the optimism of youth and the determination never to abandon a child or desert my own convictions in the face of opposition. Soon after that marvel-filled year, obstacles came into my life that postponed the college education I had so carefully planned, but I never forgot April.

I was thinking of her in December of 1999 when I finally crossed the stage in front of my parents, my husband, and most of all, my own children, and received my degree, twenty-five years later. The awesome realization that I experienced when I received my teaching certificate and faced my first real class was that it was my job to preserve the wonder and curiosity of those innocent eyes and not let living kill it. And, every time I brush my hair, I remember the wonder of April.

Oh, Josh!

Sunita Watson
Barfield Elementary School, Grade 2

Josh was diagnosed with a laundry list of secret codes by the third grade, and I was to inherit him. He liked yelling and being defiant, and for fun he kicked tables and threw fits in the cafeteria. We fourth grade teachers would regale ourselves with stories of Josh being carried out of the cafeteria by our principal.

When Josh came to me—because the principal knew "I could handle him"—he was just as mean as a wet polecat. He was making D's, which were just "Dandy" in his opinion, or provoking, "daring" me to make him "do" something. I tried treating Josh fairly and I was consistent with him. I never berated him; in fact, I became his defender. He enjoyed art, so I found a way to use that to my advantage. If he refused to do some written work or participate in a discussion, I allowed him to draw or illustrate the scenario, problem, or discussion, much as a courtroom painter visually documents the proceedings.

I'm not sure quite how it happened, if I had done something significant or of interest, but after Valentine's Day, two things had changed. First, I noticed that Josh, whose hormones must have engaged, had developed a crush on me. (OK, that's fine. Whatever gets their attention. I also have a collection of sparkly and theme-related jewelry—some that make sounds.) Second, Josh was compliant, making the grade, and dare I say, sweet? Yes, he had been transformed before my very eyes without anyone watching. Josh was helpful, friendly, and even buddied with students who needed help. By the end of the year, he was doing so remarkably well that I had forgotten he was a "problem" student.

I moved away that summer, but in the fall I returned to visit my old school. Upon entering one of the fifth grade classes where everyone was working diligently on some project, I was accosted by a medium-framed boy with newly dyed, flaming, spiky-orange hair and an earring.

"Mrs. Watson!" Josh squeezed me and grinned warmly.

"Oh, Josh!" A single tear sauntered down my cheek. I love it when that happens!

Rite of Passage

Kathy McMahan
Smyrna Elementary School, Grade 4

We have been friends forever. We were part of a close-knit circle from a small church, but we two shared many other connections. We were in marching band together as well as concert band. We were in the same classes at school. Our mothers were friends. We met her husband while still in junior high school and were all friends even before they started dating.

We earned the same college degree from the same university and both began teaching at a time when teaching jobs were difficult to come by. We were in each other's weddings. Other close friends came and went, but this friendship lasted as we went down different paths.

Even though we ended up eventually living two hours apart, the magic of long-held friendship was always there. We laughed at the little things that no one else would understand and cried deeply about each other's sorrows. We handled each other's children as if they were our own. We shared concerns, doctor's comments, and developmental milestones for our families. We valued each other's opinions and trusted each other's judgment.

People who knew us only after we were grown often asked if we were sisters. After seeing us together for even a few minutes they recognized what we had always known and perhaps had taken for granted. We even started looking like we were related.

She was the one who did a better job of keeping in touch. She sent cards for all the important events. I made better use of the telephone than I did of the mail.

Things are different now. We do not call or visit much anymore. When we do reach out, it is just not the same.

I tell myself that this is just one of the ups and downs old friends go through. Over the years there have been times when we called and visited infrequently as family and work made extreme demands. We always knew we could pick up again as soon as life slowed down. There was always an emotional connection.

I tell myself that this is one of those times, but I fear it is not.

Things changed for us when her mother was the one we gathered around to bury. The old patterns do not work anymore. The distance between us is far more than the miles. I think of her often, but I feel paralyzed and do nothing to let her know how much I miss her.

There's a sense of isolation between us. It's been a few years now since her mother passed and things are some better, but they're not good enough. When I call, I do not hear the same welcome. When I visit, we manage to recapture some of the old magic, but it does not hold. She seems removed from me. She seems so far away that I find myself reluctant to discuss the problem as

24

if that would be an intrusion on her privacy.

I feel so guilty. When her mother passed, I was in the middle of a devastating health crisis that also caused a financial crisis and was not really myself. I tried to explain, and she said she understood, but then, what else could she say. My pride was so great, and her pain was so numbing even to see that I really did not do a very good job of explaining or supporting.

I know from others that she is not her old self with them. I am not my old self either.

I wish I could have done more, explained better, been more honest about just how bad my situation really was. I did not open myself, as a real friend should. Strength and a stiff upper lip are not always good things. Pride truly does go before a fall.

We have now buried the mothers of most of the women in our circle. We've attended the funerals together for our other mothers. These were all women who had a big impact on each of our lives. We attended the funerals together, rode to the cemeteries together, laughed and cried and somehow got through it together.

We are coming closer to that time when we will be the matriarchs of our families.

Burying one's own mother is a great divide that that we all must cross. Maybe this is what is really separating us. I am almost the only one from our circle who still has her mother alive. I cannot imagine what life will be like when my mother is not here. Although I have buried many close relatives who were an important part of my life, I cannot imagine what she has gone through or really feel what she faces every day with that piece of herself missing.

Somehow we must find a way to continue our connection.

I will share this piece with her and be brave enough to start what will undoubtedly be a difficulty journey. She and I must find a way to reconnect. As we travel the uncertain path that is life, we cannot allow ourselves to lose the most precious security that comes from having a forever friend forever.

To My Dear Friend

Deborah Grady
Oakland High School, Grades 9-12

June 15, 2004

Dearest Friend,

Now that school is out I find myself sitting in of all places a classroom. The "teacher" now is the student, and of all classes I could take, I'm in a writing class (one thing I loathe more than going to the dentist). To you I will write a letter that may let you inside my soul and say things to you that only my closest friends know about me.

My summer is going well. I spend a great deal of time at the community pool. I'm the pool treasurer or one of the "Queens" of the pool. I bet you did not know that a hive could have more than one queen. As treasurer of the pool, I get to spend money. (I like to spend money even if it is not mine.) To go shopping for items to make our pool safe and comfortable is fun. Besides, I am a member of that pool also.

As treasurer I get to meet most of the members because you have to pay me in order to get a key to gain entrance to the pool. The members are such good family-oriented people. All the mothers enjoy taking time out of their busy days to bring their children to splash and frolic in the cool clear water. Mothers pack coolers filled with yummy morsels that their own children won't eat. Don't worry, their children will be fed because my munchies are better than theirs. Happy children make happy parents, or is that the other way around?

Another thing that is keeping me busy this summer is my garden. I just spent two days pulling weeds by hand. The muscles in my legs are paying for it now. I'm not complaining because I had rather be outside hearing birds chirping, frogs croaking and feeling the soft breeze passing over my dirty, sweaty body. To also hear that little voice calling out from the backdoor, "Can we go to the pool today?" I call back, " Five more minutes of weeding please!" Five more minutes turns into an hour. The little voice is back, "I'm bored mother, can we go to the pool NOW!" My how the voice has grown but no weed will prevail!

I guess I've always liked digging in the dirt since childhood. Did you ever try to dig a hole in the ground thinking you would end up in China? I did. I wonder what my mother thought watching her children from the kitchen window working diligently in one spot in the backyard knowing the whole time that we could never reach China. The only thing that was found was worms, crickets, beetles, and of course more dirt. How many hours did I spend on that hole?

I still spend hours in the dirt with a small garden each summer. I think of my garden like I think of being a mother. You sow seeds or put plants in the ground give them water, nutrients and make sure the weeds don't take over and it will bring you health and happiness. I give my children water, nutrients and love to keep the weeds away and hope they will have health and happiness throughout their lives.

Got to go for now, the weeds are calling or is that the wild cry of, "MOTHER, can we go to the pool NOW!!!!"

Thinking of you always,
Deborah

Dear Matthew

Ann Patient
Rockvale Elementary School, Grade 6

Dear Matthew,

Today, June 16, 2004, things are extremely confusing around here. There are so many unanswered questions that only you can answer. I guess where you are things are heavenly. I just felt the need to write you and tell you how special you are. I know you've heard that a lot from your grandma.

You have such a free spirit and generous heart. One that is not afraid to have fun, joke with your teacher, or give your grandma a big bear hug in front of the entire eighth grade. You have so much going for you.

I always admired you for not acting spoiled. Money and possessions never really seemed to matter to you. You eagerly shared with those who were less fortunate. Your family and friends were always at the top of your list. You always wanted to please everyone.

Over the past three years our paths have crossed many times. However, this crossing is the most difficult. How I'd love to see the big grin or hear that goofy laugh. Those images will be tucked away in my treasure chest of memories. In this crossing I don't receive the big hug or hear that your grandma is wonderful. I don't hear your ball stories, see pictures of your dad and the fish you caught, or hear that your mom is doing great and that Aunt Cynthia is good, too.

As our paths cross this time I can tell you about your family. They're all here and are not great at all. Puzzled looks, tears, and daydreaming are how I would describe them now. Your grandma is still as strong as ever, holding things together in her beautiful graceful way. She is such a blessing in your life as you are in hers. All of your friends are here to return the kindness and support you have shown them over the years. Yes, lots of confusion.

Normally when our paths have crossed it is filled with laughter and promises of a bright tomorrow. At this time there are only tears and memories. I hope that our paths will cross again someday. Instead of me showing you around and making you feel welcome you can do that for me.

As you know I always try to be a positive influence to my students and touch their lives in a special way. However, in this case, Matthew, you have touched my life as well.

Love,
Mrs. Patient

A Brick in My Foundation

Cynthia Roberts
Smyrna Primary School, Librarian

Today it gently soldiers a row of beloved books on my bookshelf at home. But, that cinnamon-colored block of clay is more than just a bookend for some profound words. It is a concrete reminder of my own foundation.

Many yesterdays ago, the Old Dunn House was my-home-away-from-home, my favorite place to be, my heaven-on-earth. Granny and Pop lived there. Actually, they more than lived there; they celebrated life there every single day. The white, clapboard house brimmed with love, and family filled its spaces. Love had been passed down in that house. My great, great-grandfather built the house after being honorably discharged from the Union Army after the war. His son raised his family there, and then my grandmother brought her new husband there to live. As a child, I could feel all of that history and those decades of love as soon as I opened the door.

It wasn't just my favorite place, though. My grandparents' children and grandchildren spent hours after hours at the Old House. We all craved its essence—family. We came for Sunday morning after-church breakfast, and we stayed for Sunday dinner. On warm summer evenings, when the ice cream freezer cranked out a pink peppermint treat, we and the night cooled down. Lightning bugs and moonlit stories captured our attention.

Sometimes I would sit in the kitchen at the old red Formica-topped table and watch Granny and her sister cook and bake together like synchronized swimmers who never came up for air. They possessed a type of reverence for what they did. Rolling out dough, dropping teacakes on the cookie sheet, and stirring Mary Ball fudge brought them as much joy as the eating of their creations brought the rest of us.

In the mid-1960's, when my grandparents could no longer afford to shear up the sagging floors and replace the rusty roof of the Old House, they determined that the best option was bulldozing. My heart broke. For several years, I went back to the vacant land, to nourish my memories and myself. In the early 1970's, I discovered some forgotten bricks in the towering weeds near where the house once lived. Those bricks were part of the foundation of a house and of a family. They represented the foundation of my life.

Today one of those bricks hugs my books on my bookshelf and reminds me of the love that enveloped me in that old house.

My Two Favorite Things

Teresa Johnson
Rock Springs Elementary School, Grade 5

In 1992, I was given a beautiful boy Yorkie.
I named him Rascal because he was kinda corky.

He loved to be with me and play until dark.
Because of his need for a companion, Sweetpea was given to be his spark.

They spend all day together waiting on my to return.
Immediately I have no concerns.

They greet me with jumps and licks.
We go outside so they can lay bricks.

At night they eat and lay at my feet.
Just to wake waiting for a treat.
Never a dirty look or a harsh word.
I have considered a third.

Rascal and Sweetpea my two favorite things.

The Wedding Vase

Holly Knox
Siegel High School, Grades 9-12

Two spouts braided into one
Desert brown, glazed by the sun
formed by the hands of Lizzie John
weathered, old, *mi corazón.*

It comes from New Mexico
home of the Navajo
We set off impulsively
A simple, short ceremony.

He was a rail-thin type of cowboy
I was studious and coy
We were educated but poor
the open road, a seductive lure.

Mesas, red rock, infinite blue sky
Shiprock, Elephant Butte, mysterious magpie
Deep out of the Canyon in Chinle, Arizona
Bid *adios* in New Orleans, Louisiana.

Green chiles, *ristras*, purple green sage
They swore we'd never make it to this age
United still, only God knows
The wedding vase of the Navajos.

The Bag

Susan Pawlowski
Walter Hill Elementary School, Grade 3

Gazing at this worn-out bag
One would never know
How it embraces my past so firmly
And pieces of myself that I cannot let go.

For some of my greatest memories
Are with my grandmother late at night
When we'd sit and read until it got so late
We'd finally have to turn off the lights.

Within the pages of these books
I escaped to the far corners of my mind
And I envisioned a world of magic and wisdom
With my grandmother's reading of each line.

Years flew by and her health began to fade
And precious memories soon perished.
Eventually all that remained
Was the frail, broken body of this woman we had cherished.

The heart so full of love finally stopped
And my only wish was to find
The books we had shared so long ago
When it was a more magical and simpler time.

The books were not in their usual place.
I searched through seventy-five years of accumulation
Until I came upon this old, shabby bag
Which I then pulled free without hesitation.

Paper-clipped on the dirty handles of this bag
Was a note in the delicate handwriting I knew.
"For Susan" I read as I exposed its contents.
The smell of dust and mothballs broke through.

On peering inside this worn-out bag I found
The books I had been hunting so frantically for.
It was if she had had the same memories as I had
From all those many years before.

So to you looking at this much-used bag
You think of something useless and tattered.
But to me it contained a beautiful, hidden treasure
Proving to me that love through reading matters.

As For Me
Jan Wadleigh
Rock Springs Middle School, Grade 8

My favorite thing?
Perhaps my wedding ring.
Or should it be the stack of books?
Piled overflowing in the yellow nook.

What is it about the music that feeds my heart?
The joy and harmony that spreads to every part –
Of my being – calming or speeding
Depending upon the task I am weaving.

Should it be my favorite children or pups?
Not them, I think, they're too much.
What about God?
To him I must yield more than a nod.

His creation, our planet, Gaia, Mother Earth
Without her, we as humans would have no birth.
My slice of magma, ash, and smoke frozen in time
Allows me to thank God for the primordial climb.

Why Sunflowers?

Lynda Newman
Smyrna Middle School, Grade 7

"But Ms Newman, why sunflowers?' the child asks in wonder. "They are SO big, so pushy. Why are sunflowers your favorite?"

The year was 1995. We had just finished our tour of Auschwitz and had boarded the bus as silent as the chambers we had narrowly escaped. We were now on our way to Berlin, the next stop on our quest to understand the Holocaust. I was desperate to work through the agony that now consumed me. I could barely breathe. I had to be alone. I sat as far removed from my fellow travelers as I possibly could.

Teaching the Holocaust had long been an integral part of my curriculum. I had leaped at the opportunity to see, to experience, to bring back the first person point of view. This would make me a better teacher and thus, would help my students. I had no idea, not an inkling, that my life would be forever changed; that what I saw, heard and felt would forever be seared on my mind and branded on my soul. Relating to my students this chapter in man's inhumanity to man would become my passion, my reason to teach.

Through my agony I heard one of my new friends say "Lyn, look out of your window." "Leave me alone" I answered, unsure as to whether or not I had spoken out loud. Several more times, each repetition more insistent than the last, the voice urged me "Lyn, look out of your window." In frustration, to silence this voice invading my private agony, I looked up. There they were - sunflowers. They were everywhere, as far as the eye could see, alive, buoyant, tenacious – alive. These sunflowers were a gift to me from on high. The evidences that had so recently been offered us of man's cruelty, his depravity, had brought me so low; I had reached the bottom of my well and was filled with despair. I was yearning, no anxious, for beauty and life. My spirit had to be revived and there they were. I took them in, with my eyes and with my heart and with my spirit. Their beauty, their size – they seemed to revel in being alive. Sunflowers. They had conquered all obstacles and had survived and, yes, even flourished. I was ready to learn more, to experience more. I was eager to continue on this journey of discovery. I had been renewed.

So how to answer the question now posed by my student? I look at him and simply say, "Sunflowers lift me up."

A Gift From My Father

Myra O'Steen
Siegel High School, Grades 9 and 11

A person's voice is a priceless treasure. I learned this at an early age. My voice was significant to my family, even when I was a young child. The place that I learned this lesson best was at our kitchen table. It was at this table that my father instituted the family council.

The rules for our family council were simple, the lessons complex. The rules were as follows: any family member could call a family council; any subject could be submitted for discussion, as long as it was respectfully presented; each family member's opinion was expected and solicited; and, sometimes, Daddy had to decide.

It truly was a life-shaping experience, to have everyone's eyes focused upon me as I shared my thoughts or ideas. As a female, I learned that I was as equally valued as my brother. As a young female, I would expect no less for the rest of my life, from any man worth knowing. As a child, I learned I had a voice that needed to be heard. As a human, it meant I should learn all I could so that I would be well informed and worthy of the attention that my voice commanded.

Some council meetings were over the trivial matters of family life. Whether we were sick of beef roast for Sunday lunch, my brother presenting his case for a later curfew, or deciding our plans for July Fourth, the family council was called upon as our tool for negotiating the rapids of family life.

Some council meetings were over much more important concerns. One in particular I will never forget. Before Christmas one year, my daddy called the family council. There was a family with three children that wanted bicycles from Santa. Life had conspired to deal some harsh circumstances to this family, and my daddy knew that three bicycles were going to be awfully hard to come by for this family. My father knew that he couldn't *really* have Christmas, if somewhere on another street in our town those children were not waking up to bikes. So, he asked us to decide if we could have less for Christmas, so that those three might have their bikes. Since I was my brother's junior by ten years, and the baby with the greatest expectations for what Santa would bring, the decision actually fell to me. I will never forget the pride my family had in me, when I decided that we should, indeed, help that family. My voice was the deciding voice. I don't remember getting one thing less for Christmas that year, but I do remember the wonderful feeling of knowing that our Western Auto Store had delivered three bicycles to those children. I don't recall receiving a single item less that Christmas, but I do remember the priceless treasure of the gift of my voice from my father, the value of which was made clear to me in that season of giving.

The Most Precious Gift

Allyson Long
Siegel High School, Grades 9-12

My most treasured possession resides inside a sealed box in the uppermost corner of a dusty closet in my home. I never open the box. I rely on pictures and memories to remind me of every detail of that which I prize most: my wedding dress. Sure, a wedding dress is a woman's most gorgeous gown. Mine was no exception. But the reason this dress transcends all of my other belongings and holds the honor of being my most treasured possession is because my grandmother made it.

My grandmother is from a large family; she learned to sew early in life. Grandma worked at several different jobs until my mother was born. When she was five, my mother cried at the thought of my grandmother going to work so Grandma just stayed home. Grandma earned money by making and altering clothes for people in town. All my life, I knew that Grandma could make anything. She made play clothes and dresses for me when I was little and could always fix anything that tore, needed hemming, or simply lost a button. I always admired her talent.

The night I became engaged a swarm of emotions and thoughts engulfed me: Who would perform the ceremony? Who would be my maid of honor? How long would I have to stand around in uncomfortable shoes? Yet the most important and pressing question in my mind was, "Will Grandma make my dress?" Nothing else really mattered. Of course, by this time my grandmother was a little older and claimed that she couldn't see as well as she used to, but I knew that for her, sewing was as natural as breathing. I persisted. She resisted. I pouted. She argued. I cried. She agreed.

The first fitting of my immaculate gown was a sight to behold indeed. My "gown" consisted of just the bodice section, which had been cut out of an old pair of dark green, scratchy curtains Grandma had lying around. I felt like the children in *The Sound of Music*. I still have that fabric with the pins still in it that Grandma used to tell herself what needed taking in and what needed letting out. Many more fittings followed. Grandma always apologized about me having to stand for so long, but I relished every moment of it. I always felt so privileged to be there, witnessing this beautiful progression unfold. Each time I saw my dress, it was always more extraordinary than I had remembered.

I remember how I felt as though my breath had been knocked out of me when I saw my finished dress. I had never seen anything so beautiful in my life, nor anything that had such history and such love behind it. I could only imagine the

36

agonizing hours my grandmother had spent bent over her work, eyes stinging and fingers aching. I envisioned her endlessly sewing buttons by hand, carefully layering folds of white satin, and gently edging the veil with a delicate ribbon. I hardly felt worthy of wearing such a beautiful gown.

I told everyone I knew that Grandma made my dress. She told no one. I boasted and bragged about it to anyone and everyone who would listen. She quietly deflected my praise. (She did, however, provide my maid of honor with detailed instructions as to how the train should be arranged at all times). Standing at the altar on my wedding day, I was surrounded—literally and figuratively—in love.

My grandmother told me weeks later that someone had remarked to her that my dress looked "just like a Vera Wang." She had smiled politely at him, having no earthly idea what that meant. When my astonished husband incredulously informed her that Vera Wang was only *the* most sought after designer for wedding gowns in the world, Grandma only looked mildly surprised and then responded modestly, "Well, it wasn't really *that* good...." But I think I did see just the faintest flicker of pride in her eyes. Although my dress now lies in that dusty box in my closet and though I haven't worn it in a number of years, I still vividly recall the feelings of awe, love, and comfort I had as I wore it. The most precious gift that my grandmother gave me was not a dress. It was a testament of her deep love for me, and more importantly, a priceless piece of herself.

Prince Albert in a Can

Tonya Hollandsworth
Smyrna Elementary School, Grade 2

My grandfather had wavy, tinsel silver hair that framed his soft blue eyes, and a tall, lanky stature that commanded everyone to look upwards as he spoke. I didn't mind his long, thin fingers or veiny hands because granddaddy was handsome. He had that "Hollywood" kind of look with strong, high cheekbones and a cleft chin. Granddaddy used a wooden crutch taller than my six-year-old self, which he tucked beneath his left arm as he walked or stood. And, he had his vices of drinking too much apple wine and smoking tobacco. Aside from this, Granddaddy didn't have much of anything else. His few possessions were kept in a tan, leather suitcase – the kind which had straps that buckled to keep it closed.

But, he did have a collection of Prince Albert cans. Shiny, red tin with silver lids all lined up against the windowsill. They were just the right size for little girl hands, and the perfect place to keep " what nots" . He'd often give me one but not before placing in a handful of pennies. CLINK. CLINK. I would take that can and shake it; listen to the rattle. Then I'd dance and twirl along with the sound.

The can would have been enough to suit me fine, but those shiny pieces of copper he put inside became my treasure. " What would they be today?" I would ponder. Perhaps old Spanish coins I had retrieved far and deep in the ocean from a sunken Pirate ship. Maybe they will be gold coins carried in the silken purse of a well-to-do aristocratic woman. Sometimes I would just use them as money while shopping in my pretend store. Oh the memories of those simple cans filled with pennies! I bet I had hundreds throughout my childhood. I would play with them until I grew bored or tired then I'd toss them away.

I was twenty-six when Granddaddy died. As he lay at rest, I placed a shiny, red tin can beside him but not before I placed in a handful of pennies. My last gift to him was his best gift to me. Prince Albert in a can sits atop my kitchen cabinet as an ever present reminder of my affection for my grandfather who didn't have much but had all a little girl needed.

I Remember

Karen Stroud
Lascassas Elementary School, Grades 6 and 7

I remember that big room filled with anxious six-year olds and more anxious parents.
And the smell of crayons and freshly-oiled wood floors.

I can see the desperate look on the curly-headed boy's face and the tears on his cheeks as his mom attempted to comfort him. And another child with an ugly-scarred arm clinging to her mom, likewise.

I remember lining up in Miss Betty Lou's office and the poignant smell of alcohol mingled with Miss Ross's squeaky voice and crying children. With knees knocking and our sleeves rolled up, prepared for the sharp prick of the needle.

I remember the blue drink box and the nickel and penny I dropped in the slot to retrieve cold refreshment. It was near the classroom filled with children who slowly shuffled past and the boy whose impeded speech I can still hear.

I remember the lunchroom and the 25-cent lunch ladeled onto green melmac trays.
Pungent kraut and wieners was the mainstay along with applesauce and steaming homemade rolls.

I can feel the stinging pop Mrs. Sims delivered to my leg to squelch chattering during nap time. And the mountain of red and blue we formed as we stacked our nap pads in the dark, damp cloakroom.

I remember how I cherished and despised that year; it was simple, yet difficult – effortless, yet drudgery. It was first grade.

Chapter Two

Connecting through Personal Thoughts

Who Am I?

Kenya Howse
Wilson Elementary School, Grade 4

I am curious, loving, faithful, yet true.
I wonder why the sky is blue.
I hear my Uncle Bobby's voice pushing me to succeed.
I see a classroom filled with children anxious to read.
I want to relax on a tropical island rendezvous.
I am curious, loving, faithful, yet true.
I pretend that some things do not bother me.
I believe my God protects me.
I touch the lives of every child I meet.
I feel for the children with no food to eat.
I worry that cancer will never have a cure.
I cry when I consider all the worldly things my daughter Kiara will endure.
I am curious, loving, faithful, yet true.
I understand that I must put things in God's hands when I have done all I can do.
I say live life to the fullest and include lots of fun.
I dream of someday receiving the love of that special someone.
I hope to break tradition and do things out of the blue.
I am curious, I am loving, I am faithful, yet true.

I Am

Carol Hawkins
Christiana Middle School, Grades 7 and 8

I am a seeker of knowledge,
 A lover of nature
  A child of God.

I wonder about people, places, and history.
I see everything though much remains a mystery.
I hear the world calling me to places to explore.
I want to know, to understand, and much more.

I am a seeker of knowledge,
 A lover of nature
  A child of God.

I pretend to be in a lakeside cabin in the rain.
I touch leaves and stone as I walk the terrain.
I believe my life is content as God oversees.
I watch the tall poplars swaying in the breeze.

I am a seeker of knowledge,
 A lover of nature
  A child of God.

I understand nothing but trust in God's guidance.
I dream of my life lived as a wondrous dance.
I say I believe, but my vision is clouded by doubt.
I hope I can walk with God day in and day out.

I am a seeker of knowledge,
 A lover of nature
  A child of God.

Ecclesia

Brian D. Wilcox
Thurman Francis Arts Academy, Grade 5

I am hopeful, melancholy, silly, imperfect.

I wonder why people wonder about life.

I hear a distant waterfall, and I missed what you just said.

I see a curtain up ahead that obscures what is beyond, but I see what shines

above.

I want to ascend a narrow path with eyes fixed upward, drawn by love.

I am hopeful, melancholy, silly, imperfect.

I pretend to be happy and lighthearted, but only sometimes.

I believe in air, whether I can see it or not.

I touch other people's lives, so I'd better mind the impression I make.

I feel fine—no, anxious; well, see doc, I've got this pain.

I worry when things are not just so.

I cry when I hear of a life transformed, of the Power that plucks a soul from

death.

I am hopeful, melancholy, silly, imperfect.

I understand that life right now is like a breath—in and out.

I say, "I've faith. There's more. I have no doubt."

I dream of what I've seen before, and maybe just a little more.

I hope. I hope. Without it, what is life?

I am hopeful,

      melancholy,

         silly,

            imperfect.

Through my Eyes

Latasha Allison
Blackman Elementary School, Grade 3

I am shy, sensitive, and skeptical.
I wonder why I question so much.
I hear the shuffling of ideas, questions, and thoughts within my head.
I see the world drifting by.
I want to stop feeding my fears.
I am shy, sensitive, and skeptical.
I pretend to be okay.
I believe that I have an inner purpose.
I touch the window and stare through the glass.
I feel lost, alone, confused.
I worry through endless hours of my days.
I cry as I sit and wonder.
I am shy, sensitive, and skeptical.
I understand that life is full of meaning.
I say that everything happens for a reason.
I dream of shedding my sorrow and walking fulfilled and free.
I hope for better days.
I am shy, sensitive, and skeptical.

I Am from America

Stacy Ryel
Smyrna High School, Grade 9

I am from grandma's backyard, barefoot summers, and waterslides.
I am from firefly war paint, bottle rocket ammunition, and wild Indian war hoops.
I am from recycled pop bottles, when they were made from glass, traded for the change to buy candy cigarettes and pop rocks.

I am from grandmother's formal parlor, patent leather shoes, and the country club pool.
I am from quiet card games, flower gardens, and polite conversations.
I am from elegant luncheons with lace collars and fine china, remembering that "children are to be seen, not to be heard."

I am from the country and the city, from poverty and wealth.
I am from Indian Time and Tea Time.
I am from mother's blood and father's blood.
I am from Native shore and foreign shore.
I am from America.

Lisa

Lisa G. Beasley
Oakland High School, Grades 9-12

Lisa
Creative, loving, giving, sad
Who loves her family, creating flower
arrangements and crafts with her girls
Who hates taking care of money issues
and other financial topics
Who fears growing old without her love
Who feels sad and lonely since Robert died
and sad her daughters will grow-up
without their daddy
Resident of Murfreesboro, Tennessee
Beasley

Insecure, but Hopeful

Kim Cing
Siegel High School, Grades 9 and 10

I am insecure, but hopeful.
I wonder what my ultimate achievement in life will be.
I hear God's sweet and patient encouragement and my own doubts.
I see myself and my family playing together, carefree.
I want to be free of worry and stress.

I am insecure, but hopeful.
I pretend that I am self-sufficient – I'm not.
I believe that God will meet *all* my needs.
I touch lives of teenagers – both at school and in youth group.
I feel undeserving of the blessings my Heavenly Father has bestowed upon me.
I worry about living my life to glorify Him and to be an example to those
around me.
I cry because I realize all of the opportunities I let slip away.

I am insecure, but hopeful.
I understand that I am not supposed to be in total control of my circumstances.
I say that I have faith in God – but do I live by that faith daily?
I dream of the day I will meet my Creator face to face.
I hope He will be able to say, "Well done, my good and faithful servant."

I am insecure, but hopeful.

The Path to Healing

Allyson Long
Siegel High School, Grades 9-12

I am Pain.
I reside in the bellies of hungry children, the eyes of mourners, and the souls of those who are suffering.
I wear filthy cloaks and diamond earrings.
My task is to thwart healing, to promote blame, and to overwhelm with guilt.
My conspirators are Pride, Stubbornness, Apathy, and Doubt.
I linger in the hearts of those who have been shattered and not yet healed.
I cast shadows over dreams and veil the eyes of Truth.

I am Hope.
I dwell in the hearts of new mothers, the minds of battle-weary soldiers, and the smiles of young children.
I dress in robes of whitest satin, embroidered with gold.
My desire is to soothe the fears and wipe away the tears of the suffering.
My sisters are Patience, Love, Kindness, and Peace.
I am always present for all who seek me but I do not enter unless invited.
I illuminate the feelings of the heart and can show you the path to healing.

Normandy

Libby Sullivan
Roy Waldron School, Grade 5

He closed his eyes.
He recalled Mom and Dad.
He tasted the root beer at the drive-in.
He remembered his grand slam.
He savored his first kiss.

He whispered a prayer.
  God, let me be brave.
  God, let me get home.
  God, don't let me fail.

He stepped to the door and jumped into the night.
He fell.
His parachute grabbed him.
He floated and then touched Earth, his cricket clutched in his hand.

He clicked and waited.
He clicked and waited.
Friend or foe,
Life or death,
Out of the night, the answer – Click.

Our Song

Melissa Dishner
Cedar Grove Elementary School, Grade 5

It's been twelve years since they began playing our song.

"Get on Your Feet"

I remember watching as the star student greeted his girlfriend before every nine o'clock rehearsal. His smiles and gestures were gentle and enduring. They seemed to share something – a mystery to me. Every Monday, Wednesday, and Friday I watched as the two strangers said their hellos sending familiar feelings of envy and hope accompanied by those resounding questions, "I wonder what that feels like?" and "Will I have ever have someone like that?"

As fate would have it, with the help of a choral master and romantic genius, we were assigned as dancing partners in the MTSU Show Choir. Dancing and singing in the legendary style of the Opryland Singers, he spun me out and reeled me tightly in as we sang, "…get up and make it happen."

-so we did

"You Deserve a Break Today"

The Wright Music Building was quiet with only a single guitar student rehearsing the lines of his jury piece and the music history listening list being heard as the library door opened and shut. Awaiting my ride from one whom I knew would not be in a hurry to see me, my knight in shining armor strolled to the scarred wooden bench opposite me in denim shorts, a spent black t-shirt, and docksiders – sole held to leather with 3 tight rounds of duct tape. He was breath-taking.

A very nervous conversation for me, but a well-managed one for him sounded something like this:

"What are you still doing here?" Probably all he could come up with for a girl like myself, I thought.

"Just waiting for my ride. He's usually a little late."

"I thought you weren't together anymore." Now how would he know that? Why would he care? "I'm sorry. My girlfriend and I just went our separate ways, too. I decided not to see anyone until God says, 'Hey you, this is it!'"

"Yeah, me too," I mumbled as if I believed the day would ever really come. Silence was heard as he accompanied me during my wait.

"Hey, I'm hungry. Would you like to get a burger at McDonald's? They're 2 for $2."

-and I did

"What I Did for Love"

It was my turn to endure the MTSU Singers alone. As the last song of the rehearsal routine suggested, I was belting out, "...won't forget, can't forget what I did for love." Little did I know outside the door stood an audience of two, one aggravated by the tardiness of my dismissal and one who, for some reason or another, was impressed and didn't understand the lack of interest voiced by the other.

"Why don't you go ahead if you want? I would love to stay and listen. I'll wait for her."

-and he did

"Breaking Up Is Hard to Do"

A time came, as it does with many, that commitment became a little scary. For three semesters we began our days with each other listening to a music history scholar advise us on the love lives of historical composers when all we were consumed with was ours. We ended our days together begrudgingly around midnight or one o'clock if we could find a study session. If not, we created our own. –too much of a good thing, I guess.

Finding yourself sitting home, alone, at four in the afternoon longing for a call can be quite uneasing – especially when you don't get it. Instead, however, I received a visit. One look at my guest told me this was not a good thing. With *Bible* in hand, my visitor did his best to explain why we needed "a break." My discernment of the situation told me he was just wrong.

I spent the introductory period of the next semester memorizing his schedule, devising a plan to be wherever he was, talk to those he spoke to, and do what he would do. With a little pondering I could explain why an education major was quietly studying in the RIM department, why I decided to get in shape and begin walking with his friend whom I found positively annoying, and even why I needed to stop by the Duds-n-Suds when I had no laundry. Yes, staying away was painstaking.

-but we did

"Bella Siccome"

The beautiful thing about true love is it never goes away completely. Per his request, my escort, of whom I was forlorn, began appearing in strange places. Sporadic appearances became the norm, and our time together was restored. One of our first outings was a Nashville Opera engagement at an upscale bookstore. The sight of him in his navy blazer, khakis, and red paisley tie was an answer to my hopes and prayers as I became enthralled with his voice. Those sitting around me were involved in his music as well, minus the lapses taken for quick sips of champagne. None of these onlookers really understood that the Italian lyrics and melodic lines were meant for the simply dressed college girl sitting on the front row. This was clearly the beginning of another chance at love for us to take.

-so we did

"She Was a Brick House"

Fun. Those people come along that you can just sit back and enjoy. Relax. Laugh. An *Hakuna Matatah* type. He was one of those. Friends and family loved to be with him, and strangers were intrigued by him. Some crazy stunts were only for the reactions. For example, his best friend loved to take him skiing only to have him stand on the ski deck and "bust a gut" singing <u>The Barber of Seville's</u>, "Largo al Factorum" for passers-by to hear. Family was entertained as he mimicked my father calling the shots during a Sunday afternoon NASCAR race – something my sisters and I could never get by with doing. Just for fun, my mother and older sister would get juicy smooches or pats on the behind. The young, daring, debonair could always put a smile on your face, and his timing was incredible. A blah day in class or a discouraging financial analysis could be scraped from my plate with a serenade of "Brick House" accompanied by his own version of dirty dancing.

-and he did

"Stars and Stripes Forever"

Anticipation built as the hometown crowd gathered at Patriot Park for the July 4, 1994, fireworks extravaganza. His family joined us for dinner and the show. Deep down I desired to hear the big question, but realized his romantic spirit would never allow such a moment in this setting. Then it happened. We were alone on the concrete path. Dodging kids unsupervised by a parental figure and latecomers scurrying for a good grassy seat, we held tightly to each other's hand. In the distance a quaint gazebo lay in our path as we were beaten by a league of children playing super heroes.

"Oh well. I guess we should head back anyway," he announced. That was it. I stopped wondering.

The fireworks were picking up speed and intensity as they blasted into the smoky sky during the finale.

"Look at the guy over there," he requested.

"What guy?" There were thousands of them from my vantage point.

"You need to stand up to see him," he pleaded.

"No. Everyone else is sitting. I am not going to stand up."

"Just stand up. Nobody's paying any attention to you."

"No. I'm fine," I demanded.

From behind me I heard his sister, an elementary school teacher who could send anybody to the corner, call, " Melissa, stand up!"

"What!?!" Exasperated, I finally followed the instructions given. At that point I didn't care if everyone did see me. What could be so important? Then I knew.

My knight in shining armor was there on one knee; ring in hand, laughing at the typical stubborn ways of the one with whom he had fallen in love. At that moment the other 4,000 people disappeared, and it was just the two of us forever.

-and we are

And they're still playing our song.

Love Is...

April Holland
Buchanan Elementary School, Kindergarten

Love is...
> passion
> unity
> devotion
> affection
> loyalty
> faithfulness
> unwavering
> precious
> honorable

Love
  gives
    life
      meaning.

A Mother in Waiting

Lisa Kegler
Wilson Elementary School, Grade 3

My favorite thing right now is an angel holding a baby. I received it as a Christmas gift from one of my students. Why is this precious statue so significant? To know this answer I must tell you my story.

I am a mother in waiting.
I wonder why some women who really want to have children can't have them.
I hear a still small voice comforting my heart and my empty arms.
I see hope and expectation.

I am a mother in waiting.
I pretend to smile at baby showers and at mothers with bulging stomachs while inside crying, wishing it were me.
I believe in miracles. I believe when it's time for my blessing I will receive.
I touch a baby's warm body, its tiny appendages, along with the love and dependence a child has for its mother.
I feel emotional; almost out of control.
I worry that maybe God's will for me does not include me bearing a child but rather to 'mother' all the youth I come in contact with.
I cry often. Especially after baby showers, or when I remember the three lives I carried for a short time.

I am a mother in waiting.
I understand that all things work for good to them that love God; I truly love Him.
I say I would love to experience a full pregnancy and bring a life into the world and home to my loving family! I also say, let the Lord's will be done.
I dream of finding out I'm pregnant and thanking God for doing the impossible.
I hope I'm not being ungrateful and unthankful for all the miracles I have already been given.

I am a mother in waiting.
After reflecting I have realized I am already a mother. A mother is someone who takes care of a child. I do that every day. Although it is my true heart's desire to bring forth a child, God has already answered my prayers. The angel holding her baby reminds me of what God has already done, what He can do, and what He will do.

My Feelings As An Adult Writer

Ynetia Avant
Lascassas Elementary School, Grade 2

My thoughts are never-ending,
But I don't know what to put on paper.

I feel malnourished as a writer,
As if I haven't been properly fed.

I fear that I'm not writing correctly,
But so what, I write anyway.

My thoughts race through my mind,
And I have so much to say.

It's like therapy; I get to let it all hang out,
And finally write it all down.

I can take a cleansing breath,
Knowing it's no longer bottled up inside.

My pen and paper now know my innermost thoughts!

Writing

Latasha Allison
Blackman Elementary School, Grade 3

Pen up,
Pen down
I hold my pen and stare back down.
What do they want?
What can I do?
Writing isn't always a fun thing to do.
Thoughts are racing in my head,
But "Oh, my goodness, I'm out of lead!"

Poetry

Myra O'Steen
Siegel High School, Grades 9 and 11

Poetry concisely expresses much
With rhyme, imagery, meter and such.
I love to read it, but writing it is hard,
After all, I am not, "The Bard."

The Affair

Michelle Delaney
Christiana Middle School, Grade 7

My interest in words began at a very early age. I was one of those precocious tots whose ability to use multi-syllabic words in their contextual correctness would amaze and delight the adults in my midst, reinforcing my desire to have a vocabulary worthy of envy. Being a voracious reader from an equally early age, I had discovered the factor that developed my infatuation with words into a full-blown love affair. I found in words a magical rhythm and cadence; a tango staccatoed its way across some pages while a waltz graced its way across others. I found the foreign caress of words on my tongue that brought with them the exotic sounds and textures that mimicked their origin. Rolling a particularly tasty treat around on my tongue, feeling it trip against my teeth, rattling my palate, making it as sweet as any wine to be tasted has given me many a heady intoxication. I am fascinated with the capturing of just the perfect word for the perfect moment; I will traverse the pages of a thesaurus in anticipation of the discovery. My fascination leads to an appreciation of the seriousness of words, the lexicon; but also an enjoyment of the silly and absurdness that can surround them like flibberty-gibbet. Perhaps a testament to the power of words is the endless stream of new creations that permeate our vernacular with our need to express the new innovations that are constantly becoming a part of our consciousness. Words can mask our anger, disappointment, or frustration into a semblance of an understanding we neither feel nor possess the immediate ability to acknowledge. Words can bring us to the brink of tears, ease our grief and sorrow, and bridge two souls in a single unifying thought. Words can woo two lovers across the span of time and distance, and unite them for that moment in which one can almost feel the light caress of their breeze across a cheek. Words will forever be the great love of my life to treasure, nurture, and foster while relishing in the languidness of our affair. By the way, has anyone seen today's New York Times Sunday Crossword?

Lost Love

Malinda Elledge
Smyrna Middle School, Grade 7

After I had been married for a few years, I started to think about all of the boys I left behind when I took those sacred vows of eternal devotion to one, and only one, man. What did I miss out on when I became Mrs. Scott Elledge and moved to the thriving metropolis of Smyrna, Tennessee? What adventures could have been had? What fame? What fortune? Being a research-oriented English major, I decided to find out for myself what I had given up.

First, I looked up Neil. He was the first guy I was ever serious about. Actually, he was the first, the third, and the fourth guy I was ever serious about. (The fourth time I dumped him. That makes it better, right?) Neil was a musician, a talented pianist, and vocalist who aspired to great heights. I believed in him wholeheartedly. I even bragged to the lead singer of Def Leppard that Neil was going to be a huge star some day. Did I miss out on a life of world tours, magazine interviews, and music video cameos? No. Neil is a farmer. A chicken farmer. In Arkansas.

Next, I decided to check on Evan. Evan was the star rugby player at my high school – the only freshman to make it onto the varsity team in the history of the academy. (I don't really know how long that is, but Teddy Roosevelt signed the cornerstone, so I'm thinking it was a long time.) He was handsome, charming, and destined for fame as an international rugby star. I heard he had gone to college on a rugby scholarship, so I tried to find out what team he signed with. Tried and failed. I found Evan at the Ringling Brothers Barnum and Bailey website. He is a clown. A circus clown. He wears funny clothes and makeup.

I didn't bother looking up any of my other lost loves. I was afraid of what I might discover. Instead, I ran straight for my husband. I thanked him for being a computer programmer, for living in Smyrna, Tennessee. I held him tightly in my arms, and begged him to promise me again that we will be together for eternity.

I Remember

Lisa G. Beasley
Oakland High School, Grades 9-12

I Remember
I remember when my true loved died.
And how he woke me up with a squeeze of my hand at 3 A. M.
I remember when he smiled at me in the dark of the night.
I remember the sounds as he tried to speak.
I remember how I removed his mask for him to speak to me.
And how he said, "I love you, Lisa" and blew me a kiss.
I remember the kiss was not enough, so I leaned over his bed for another kiss.
I remember we smiled and expressed "good night" and "see you in the morning."
And I fixed his mask on his face once more so he could breathe easy again.
I remember going to sleep beside his bed and grasping his hand.
I remember waking up at 5 A.M. and watching him breathe;
I remember thinking he is resting now, how peaceful he is.
And then I remember realizing something is wrong.
I remember looking closer and knowing he is gone.
I remember the machine sound as it pushed air into Robert's body.
And I remember that time slowed as the doctors and nurses said he had passed.
I remember the day when my true loved died and the world continued.

My Baby MICAH

Camille Gray
Central Middle School, Grade 7

Her Smile
Her Laughter
Her Tears
Her Joy
Her Pain
Her Love
I will never enjoy
My baby is gone to heaven above
to sit with her father in peace and love.

I Remember...

Kay Starrett
Riverdale High School, Grades 9 and 11

I remember...it is a Saturday that begins as most Saturdays in March generally do – one soccer game right after the other immediately followed by a trip to Kroger to endure the deafening screams of undisciplined children badly in need of a nap coupled with my children's continuous "Can I have this?" Will this rushing never end? Will I ever have a moment to myself?

Well, as luck has it my children are invited to accompany friends for the remainder of the afternoon. I AM FREE!!! Off I dash to hit the sales at Dillards and many other shops I would never dream to patronize with my children in tow. I prance from rack to rack thinking only of myself and of the great joys of this shopping excursion for one. In the recesses of my mind lingers my close friend Guilt gently whispering, "Shouldn't you be using some of this time to visit your mother at the rehab center?" I quickly flick Guilt from my shoulder with the excuse that I will be having dinner with Mama tomorrow and continue pillaging the piles of sale items.

Like other sinful pleasures, this too must end, and reality replaces my euphoria. A dash to the video store, a whiz through the Dominos drive-thru, and I am back in the folds of my loving family for our scheduled Saturday Family Movie Night. I do not remember what the movie was or what toppings were on the pizza, but I do remember the phone call that followed, the call that would change my life forever.

I answer the phone with the typical, casual "Hello" only to be greeted by the voice of a stranger. By the time I understand what is happening the caller has three times repeated, "Your mother has taken a turn for the worse, and we need you to immediately come to the emergency room." After several futile attempts to gain more information I jump in the Land Rover and am once again off to the emergency room.

You see, my mother is 76 years old, has many health problems, and has spent many hours in our local emergency room. This time I am alone, but my only sister is also in route from her side of town. This trip I am thinking, "What is it this time?" or "What idiot ER doctor will once again prove himself completely useless?"

My sister and I arrive almost simultaneously. As we trudge through the emergency room doors, we have no idea what will greet us. As we question the nurses at the ER station we receive the heart stopping, mind numbing phrase, "Will you please wait in this room and the doctor and paramedic will be in to speak with you shortly. We enter the room. I see a couch, chairs, a phone – and still such emptiness. I refuse to allow my mind to dwell on the gnawing realization that has begun to seep into my consciousness. Where is my mama? What is going on?

As the doctor enters I could have recited her speech with as much clarity as she due to the many summer mornings of ER reruns on TNT:

"When your mother arrived she had no heart beat. We used all available technology and exhausted all of our capabilities but were unable to restart her heart. I'm sorry but your mother died. Is there anything we can do? Do you have any questions we can answer?"

The inevitable silent pause. The quiet discussion. The phone calls home and to close relatives. Still more silence. What do I do now? Where do I go? More silence. My husband Jim, my children and my nieces arrive and we begin our trek down the long, brightly lit hall. I remember the smell of antiseptic, the flash of people, the downcast eyes. The door opens and there she lay. Quiet, serene, cold. How could she already be so cold? I hold her hand. I kiss her forehead. I touch her hair.

I'm so sorry, Mama. Why wasn't I there? Why didn't I come today? Why did I let you go through this alone? I should have been there. No, I SHOULD NEVER HAVE LEFT YOU THERE! You would have been there for me to wipe away the pain and make me smile. Never again will I hear your laughter, smell you pickling beets, taste your fried peach pies, or hear you ask my Katie if she's "still your girl". I let you down.

Inevitably my arch nemesis Guilt has returned with a power so intense that he seems impossible to vanquish. I try to deny him but still he lingers. Go away. Stop doing this to me. I make many excuses to the omnipresent Guilt but to no avail. He stays. When will I forgive myself? When will I finally give this back to God? I once again am able to pray, "Please take this from me, God. Please release my heart from this prison. He has not answered yet... or maybe, just maybe I am simply not listening.

My Connection to Myself

Lisa Ezell
Christiana Middle School, Grade 8

A path of rocks
One to the old coop
The other to the barn
Old pictures show those rocks clearly.
The chickens saw to that.
Now grass has all but covered them.
The tree, that all are sure is dead every year,
    blooms once again like a joke.
The flowers seem sad and do not grow like before.
I close my eyes and see these mental pictures.
There she is a long apron carrying baby chicks and brown eggs.
He is khaki pants and long sleeves leading the mule to the field.
I hear the songs that were surely sung while the crops were picked
And later their laughter around the endless table pulled outside at noon.
I think I smell the homemade bread she surely baked that morning.
I taste the meats of the animals stored in the smokehouse.
Kittens are lounging near the milk cans, the hounds sleep under the trees,
    and the cows slap away the flies with their tails.
These are only stories stored in my mind connecting me to them.
Now, my eyes unclosed, I find myself standing before an empty house, a
collapsing barn,
    overgrown fields, and neglected blackberry bushes.
Why does leaving this place feel like I am deserting a major part of myself?
I absolve myself saying, "I never even knew them."
Some time later I trim her plant that now grows in my yard with a tool once his.
I tie a knot like he must have.
I wear his gloves.
I touch the yellowed card on which she wrote her recipe for the meal I lay on
my small
    table.
And I finally am illuminated.
I am leaving the place, not the people…. not the connection to myself.

The Day My Life Began

Delores Vance Lannom
Buchanan Elementary School, Grade 1

The beginning of life is not always when a life begins. My life began the first day I attended university. Education was a part of a world that did not include my family. Education was important to my family; we just didn't participate in formal education. My grandfather had a second grade education, my father quit after his eighth grade year, and my mother finished the eleventh grade. I did not know a single person who had a college education.

To provide a greater understanding of me, you should know that I was born into a family of sharecroppers in Tennessee in 1957. I have only vague memories of my grandfather. My Daddy would say that he talked funny and many years passed before I realized that he spoke with a Scottish accent. When I began first grade in a small rural school, the importance of school was subtle but strong. My sister and I never missed school and the best grades were always expected. I remember a very scary day when my sister brought home her report card and her teacher had written a lower case "a" for her grade. My father was very upset because she did not make the best grade. She tried to explain to him that an "a" was the best grade that you could make. He did not agree and told her that the next grade that came home had to be a capital A. She had to bring home all of her textbooks every night for the six-weeks. When I was an adult, a lady at my church told me that when she was in school students did receive a capital A and lower case "a" that was like our A and A-today.

When I began college it was with great fear about my belonging and my ability to accomplish that great unknown that we called higher education. Higher education was for other people in other situations who were more deserving. My first course was in the summer after my graduation a week earlier. I was in a class with many "real teachers" returning to student status for the summer to update their certification. I was seventeen years old and many of these ladies were already in their fifties or sixties. They let me know very quickly that I did not know much and that I was probably unaware that I did not know anything yet. When the summer semester was over and I had six semester hours on my transcript, I remember thinking I can do this. However, I quickly finished a degree in education in three years at Middle Tennessee State University because I was always afraid that someone would stop me and ask me why are you here. I realized that higher education was the same as any other education. It involved a willingness to learn and a desire to know more about the world I lived in. Today I have a master's degree and an added thirty graduate hours. My sister has a degree in accounting. I have two nieces with degrees in education and human relationships. I have a daughter with a degree in elementary education and another daughter pursuing a degree in secondary education.

When I think back to those ladies that first semester in 1975 and their message of my ignorance about life, I realize that I really was ignorant. Ignorance keeps people in places and situations where they are not happy nor at their best. Sometimes, I think back to that young girl and I wonder who she was. Where did she go? I am comfortable in the world that I built combining my southern, rural past and my world today. Even though I am rich in knowledge about my world and many trivial facts today that is not the true education I received. My true education happened inside of me. It included an acceptance of myself as a worthy person with much to give as I educate others in my world.

Untitled

David Summar
Blackman Middle School, Grade 8

I remember lying paralyzed on the bed or the living room sofa,
Crumpled like so many forgotten wads of paper tossed just past the trash can,
Staring at the spaces where the woman
Who was my wife
Sat cross-legged, bespectacled, scratching out silvery poems;
Or crouched over a keyboard, banging out brilliant critiques of 14th century
mystics.

I remember timeless times
When my eyes were tear-streaked windows,
And my chest was choked with the smog of sorrow;

I remember missing the redolent scents of spinach and white beans simmering
too hot on the stove.
And the dirt-smeared hands wiping sweat from her brow as we worked
The garden that would bloom
Wild, lush, out-of-control:
The garden that would stiffen and freeze
Solid in its premature winter.

I remember not remembering,
When experience fogged over and the windshield would never wipe clear,
When each day peeled off like a limp, wet blanket
To reveal another day that peeled off like a limp, wet blanket,
When the days were nothing more than interludes of sleep and work.

And somewhere I remember those ghosts, with their time-rotted faces,
fading back into nothingness;
Those images receding like a penciled sketch invisibly erased and dusted off the
paper of my mind's remembering eye.

I remember seeing past the dripping window panes,
And the fog lifting from my chest,
A final exhalation of memories too noxious to persist.

I remember slipping free from that last limp, wet blanket
And finding my legs weak but able;

I remember dropping the crumpled scraps of paper into the trash can and
stepping back into time.

Chapter Three

Connecting through Fond Memories

Fond Memories

Ginger Adcock
Thurman Francis Arts Academy, Grade 6

I remember climbing into my mom's lap and reading to her for the first time. I was four and excited about my new skill. She held me tight with pride shining through.

I remember sitting on Aunt Carolyn's front porch with family saying everything or nothing at all. It was a comforting place of acceptance and love.

I remember swimming in the lake as the hot sun beamed down and the sound of laughter that surrounded me. Splashing in the water, while our skin became brown as biscuits.

I remember playing all day without a care in the world— running, jumping, hiding. We gallivanted all over the neighborhood until we heard mother's call "Dinner's ready; come home, ya'll."

I remember meeting my husband for the first time and the sense of knowing it was right. He looked at me and smiled. That was all it took for I could see the love already there.

I remember my daddy holding me and asking "Are you sure?" before escorting me down the aisle to give me away. He was worried he was losing me but that fear is gone because I will always be the apple of his eye.

I remember the feeling of my first baby's kick and how each tiny foot felt. During the football game, that was only the beginning. Jenner has never stopped but strives to go faster and further than the day before.

I remember hearing the word "mama" with understanding in Mazzy's eyes and the feeling of joy in my heart. She looked at me with a smile like she could do it all along.

I remember sensing Jesus telling me this is right and I am where I am supposed to be. He told me to quit questioning but to trust. After all, he does know best.

Lastly, I remember the warm embraces and hugs given each day. With the love given, we grow closer to one another.

Childhood Memories

Carol Hawkins
Christiana Middle School, Grades 7 and 8

I remember children everywhere, always present, crying, laughing, fighting, and teasing, but always a playmate around.

I remember sliding down grass-covered hills on cardboard boxes. It was the closest we came to sledding during California winters near the coast.

I remember road trips in "Old Betsy," our family car, as we visited family and learned about famous places and history - crack of dawn departures in our pajamas.

I remember singing in the car with Dad leading all of us while Mom got the words and the kids in order. Then to get us quiet they offered a dime for the first to spot the ocean.

I remember, "Jimmy's looking at me," whined by my sister and me. Only years later were we able to explain that our fear was the torment we knew he was plotting.

I remember Mom laughing and talking while visiting with family and friends – her chance for adult contact after confinement with the latest baby and a houseful of children.

I remember Dad on the move, building, fixing, talking, or asleep in his chair. My Mom said he only had two speeds – stop and go.

I remember watching TV with the family especially *The Wonderful World of Disney,* before and after color, and the *Wizard of Oz,* with Susan hiding from the witch.

And Dad was often found behind the set fiddling with the dials and tubes. The picture was never quite right for him. We tired of faces always changing from red to green.

I remember family cookouts over bonfires and grills. We older ones remember Danny, who stomped his marshmallow as it flamed because he'd never done it before.

I remember playing outside in the creek until dark, catching horsetails, water skimmers, frogs, and after we moved to Tennessee, crawdads.

I remember treats to the drive-in movies – Dad and Mom with seven kids in our VW bus with a couple of our own paper grocery bags full of popcorn.

I remember brothers in trouble – always hearing Mom call Jimmy then Johnny and on through the list. Even with the grandchildren, she starts with my brother Jimmy.

Mostly, I remember activity and children always present. Now, at family gatherings our children often request the stories of our misadventures. They have many favorites, which we repeat with laughter and teasing as if we were kids again. Their generation's stories are being added to the list.

I Remember

Tonya Hollandsworth
Smyrna Elementary School, Grade 2

I vividly remember the twisting, unbearable pain. Gripping my husband's hand until my knuckles were white, my legs writhing to and fro. All I could do was faintly cry, "Oh God, oh God." Part of me was squeezing his hand so tightly because I wanted him to feel some pain too. At times, I even had the urge to slap him smack across his face. I guess I thought if I could throw out some pain of my own it might have made me feel better?

I remember welcoming a six-inch needle to my back. At no other time in my life had I the desire to be poked with needles nor the stomach for it, but with the fervor of an addict I begged for it. The warm, tingly rush of the anesthesia filled my lower spine and my body collapsed from its rigid poise against the pain. The fight was over as it succumbed to the drug. Feeling such relief, or perhaps exhausted from the onslaught, I fell into a restful sleep. Other than a few interruptions by the nurse, I slept like a baby for hours.

I remember with muffled ears I could hear that someone was trying to wake me. I opened my eyes, blurred by sleep to see the nurse. "Wake up Hon. It's time to start," she whispered. All at once doubts and apprehensions filled my mind. "I'm not sure I'm ready. Oh, but you can't turn back. You have no choice. You've got to do this," I thought to myself. I felt like a first time parachutist about to leap.

I remember the feeling of prickly pins against my legs as my husband and the nurse each lifted one. They felt like five hundred pound weights, but I could see that they were still my skinny legs. With adrenaline pumping, I raised my upper body up. I faced my fears and with the might of a Trojan warrior I pushed! My first few attempts were unsuccessful. One, two, three, four …
Eyes squinted and teeth clinched, I pressed on. Five, six, seven… "Lord, give me strength. Give me might," I prayed. Eight, nine…
"I'm going to do this! I don't want any help from the doctor," I stubbornly voiced in my head. Then with enough force to move a house off its foundation, I pushed!

I remember being a part of this very surreal event. Have you ever felt as though you've come outside of yourself and you are looking on as a spectator? Some events, some experiences are so powerful, so life-changing that perhaps one's psyche cannot assimilate it all at once. I remember thinking, "This is miraculous. It is beyond human ability. Not only have I just witnessed God's hand at work but I am a part of it!" I was right on the edge of this world and heaven, briefly living between the two realms.

I vividly remember her first cry – it was the breath of life. Placing her on my belly, I reached to cradle her. My husband and I both tearfully grasped the tiny hand of an angel. "She is perfect. She is beautiful," we proudly repeated over and over. Suddenly, I knew exactly how God loves me. He loves His child (me) the way I love my own – without condition and undying.

I remember thinking how petty and short was the pain I endured.

Nina

Cynthia Roberts
Smyrna Primary School, Librarian

I remember her round-the-waist, cheek-to-cheek welcome as I stepped through the door into her kitchen.

I remember her stovetop always working overtime—okra frying, salmon patties sizzling, green beans simmering, and potatoes biding their time until just right for mashing.

She saved the hot "potato water" to add to her smooth milk gravy, stirring gently to dislodge all the crusty drippings that clung to the skillet after the color and the crispness of the salmon met her expectations.

I remember the warmth of her oven promising us fresh biscuits with tops as golden as the baby in the Coppertone commercial.

Perfect red tomatoes, still warm from the summer sun, already graced the table. Peeled and sliced for breakfast, dinner, and supper, they were a homegrown delicacy that went with everything.

I remember the little white metal stool that she always pulled up to the table for the youngest child there—ever hopeful that a child would come so that she could entertain and be entertained after the meal.

She moved from the table to the kitchen like a gentle wave, buttering biscuits and finding favorite jelly for everyone—apple, strawberry, blackberry, or muscadine — made from fruit she just couldn't let go to waste. She poured our sweet tea and hot coffee as smoothly as a waitress.

I remember her feeding even the tiniest toddler among us biscuit and coffee. The soft biscuit soaked up the creamy coffee, first doctored with a large dose of sugar. From toddler stage on, we begged for coffee and always got it.

I can hear her say, "Now, ya'll, just leave those dishes in the sink. My favorite pastime is doing dishes, and that'll give me something to do once you're gone. Go visit now."

I remember the faded, homemade, yellow-checked curtains at the window, no longer right for my kitchen; but a granddaughter's hand-me-down handiwork was always perfect for hers. Those curtains framed her view to the world beyond the kitchen, the place she'd rather be, and the place that called her even more than the dirty dishes in the sink.

I remember her place beyond the window—peonies, tulips, zinnias, gladiolas, irises, lilies, cannas, roses, petunias, peppers, squash, and tomatoes.

I remember her. I remember Nina.

Memories Flood Me

Missy Smigielski
John Colemon Elementary School, Grade 4

Do you ever go back in time and just remember?

I remember kindergarten and being crowned Queen for the day and how powerful it made me feel. I remember being a tomboy and trying to outrun every boy on the playground. I remember my sister and me curled up in bed as our dad read to us night after night. I remember fishing with Gramps, and frog gigging with dad. I remember attending church three times a week, and going to all night gospel singings with my mom dressed in fancy dresses and fishnet hose. I remember the outcome of getting in trouble, my Mimi's fly swatter. I remember mowing cornfields, feeding catfish, picking up rocks at rock festivals, and potting seedlings of new plants on the farm. I remember meeting Mike at the Student Center, working together in the college cafeteria, and how blue his eyes were. I remember connecting with the Polish culture of my husband's family: grand traditions of Notre Dame, Polish foods, dancing polkas, language spoken in Polish by my father-in-law. I remember the birth of our children, Matthew and Rachel, and how they became the joy of our lives, our very existence.

As time passes, my memories flood me like sand in an hourglass slowly pouring out.

I Remember

Melissa Ball
Central Middle School, Grade 8

I remember being picked up from school in an already crowded car. Leather seats, cold under my bottom, soon warmed up as the body heat from five other children and my Mimi traveled quickly to the windows and fogged them.

I remember my throat burning slightly as Mimi's cigarette smoke trickled over to the backseat and filled my lungs. Loud, raucous noise reverberated through my ears as each of us tried to dominate the conversation and relay the day's events.

I remember the long drive from the city school to my grandparent's farm in the country, the feeling of freedom washing over me as we pulled into the long driveway. My cousins, sister, brother, and I all pushing to be the first one out of the car ~ free to run wild while cold winter air crisped our clothes and reddened our noses.

I remember my Mimi finally calling us all in for dinner. As we entered the house, the soft warm glow from the kitchen and the smell of country fried everything entered my soul and comforted me in a way that I have never felt since my childhood. She was the glue of our family ~ the center of it all.

I remember the smell of the hospital and the feeling of desperation. I remember thinking two weeks was not enough time to say goodbye to the woman who held us all together. I remember anger, frustration, and hatred as she was stolen from us by the most cunning and cruel culprit ~ Cancer.

I remember thinking life would not, could not go on without her. But as the old saying goes, time does heal all. The sun did rise the next day, and the day after that. There are still times when I miss her so much that I can barely breathe, but I remind myself that someday I will see her again, and not just in my dreams.

9.29.01

Cary Eugene Holman
Homer Pittard Campus School, Grade 5

It would be the day that would forever change my life.
Oh, for it was my Wedding Day, and how I will always remember.

The morning came. Sickness began to creep upon my body as though
I had just been flooded by a host of angry critters. Yes, I do remember.

Yet realizing the day would continue, I drenched myself with the flow of hot
running water and liquid body soap. As I continued, I constantly stated,
"I can do this, I can do this." I remember! I truly remember.

The time had come to get dressed, eat a snack, dash the cologne, get a towel,
say a prayer, and then to enter the church. It's just like yesterday; I remember.

The doors opened, tears began to fall, stiffness paralyzed my body, yet I
continued as the music penetrated softly through the air and audience listened
and looked on. This I do remember.

When at last, my little princess was to enter the room no appearance came, only
the sound of soft music and a sweet voice. I heard these words: "I've dreamed
of becoming your bride." It was my wife to be and that I truly remember.

First prayer, scripture, songs, vows, and then the words "I do." I did it! I made
it! I was now married to the woman I loved. I remember.

Oh, how I remember the day, the day that would change my life forever.
I remember; yes, I do remember! 9.29.01–I will always remember.

Unforgettable Memories

Teresa Johnson
Rock Springs Elementary School, Grade 5

Do you have a memory that takes you back to your childhood? I remember being a kid with fond memories of visiting my grandmother. I remember the long, winding, roller coaster car trips to my grandmother's house in Hermitage. To a kid, Antioch to Hermitage, while detouring the main roads, seemed as if we were on a trip to Mars. I remember being the marshmallow squeezed tightly among three older siblings. I remember bounding out of the car to ease the urge to vomit.

I remember looking around excitedly at the enormous, full-shaded yard and wondering what I should do first walk: "Chung King", my grandmother's Pekinese dog; climb the huge oak tree, or visit in the barn with my Uncle Pappy who whittled intricate horses out of wood even though he had a terrible shake from Parkinson's Disease.

I remember doing all those unforgettable things, especially the dinners where my grandmother made her steamy mashed potatoes baked with cheese on top that would string when scooped out with a spoon. Even though I miss every unending road trip to my grandmother's house, I still remember those unforgettable moments I had that make me feel like a kid again.

I Remember Chicken Feeding Time

Mary Powers
LaVergne Primary School, Grade 2

I remember the cadence of sounds from the cackling of chickens and oinking of pigs on Grandma and Grandpa's farm back in North Carolina.

I remember feeding the chickens with wilted leaves from the pendulous branches of the towery weeping willow.

And when it was chicken feeding time, the time for their regular meal, I thought of Granny.

I remember Granny, my great-grandmother, with her old-timey sunbonnet enveloping her sweet, withered face.

I remember catching glimpses of silvery wisps, the hair that peeked around the edges of her bonnet as if playing a game of hide-and-seek.

And how her apron adorned her waistline and was filled with grains of hard, yellow corn.

I remember Granny scooping a handful of corn from her apron and then sowing them onto the ground where eager chickens waited for their meal like swooping vultures wait for the dive.

I remember watching the grains of corn send out their own little smoke signals as they peppered the dusty ground.

And that was the signal, the great race would begin as the chickens barreled over one another in order to gulp down each parched grain, as if it were their last meal.

But the best thing I remember about chicken feeding time was when Granny invited ME to scoop out a handful of corn from her apron and join in the feeding frenzy!

Cherish

Brian D. Wilcox
Thurman Francis Arts Academy, Grade 5

I remember my mother sometimes more than my brothers do because they were
so young.

I remember sweet, red, juicy strawberries one summer enjoyed at home. Most
fruits this soft are silent when they're munched at harvest's peak, but not
my mother, no not her. We heard her crunch, crunch, crunch!

I remember the neglected violin under my parents' bed. She hadn't played it
since childhood. Sometimes we peeked inside the dry, cracked leather
case and stroked the blue velvet inside and wondered how she'd make it
sound if a string or two were replaced.

And yet she brought music into our home; from a time-worn, borrowed upright
came Joplin, Chopin and more. Two younger brothers and I myself
played an instrument and sang.

I remember I was not like my father—silent, stoic, and strong. While riding in
the car one day with mother and just me—we were almost home—I said,
"I think I talk too much." "Oh, honey, no you don't." Her eyes were sad,
but I wasn't like my Dad.

I remember the anguish my mother betrayed when my anger flashed white hot
toward one of my younger brothers over some perceived injustice done.
After the moment had passed she said, "It scares me when you look that
way; that's not the boy I know."

I remember that she began making unexplained trips to the doctor. We didn't
speak of those things, but three boys began to wonder.

I remember my father had choices to make—go to Stanford or stay local.
Stanford, they decided, would take the mother too far from the boys.

I remember with what peace she lay in that bed, losing ground each day in the
struggle for life. She still maintained her grace. She had firm faith that
her heavenly Father would stay close by her three young boys, keeping
evil at bay.

I don't remember any prayer she prayed,
But I know that a mother's prayers—
my mother's prayers—got a special escort right to the throne,
and into the heart of God. Cherished for eternity.

Remembering Why

Kelly Young
Rock Springs Middle School, Grade 7

I remember looking over your shoulder while you eloquently shaped your words.
    Each letter slanting just so.
    Each word flowing from your right hand.
    Each sentence perfectly straight on the stark-white page.
Looking at your face and smiling, because your tongue was always in your cheek when you wrote.
    I wanted to have that same handwriting.

I remember hearing your voice Saturday mornings, even before the birds sang in my ears or the sun shone in my sleepy eyes.
    Each call getting louder.
    Each warning in my head.
    Each time snuggling further and further under my warm blanket.
Hearing those dreaded words even today, "Rise and shine! You're missing the best part of the day!"
    I wanted to scream.

I remember my heart breaking the day you decided to leave.
    Each excuse another brick around my heart.
    Each promise a blur.
    Each moment of silence when the door shut.
Telling myself that I would be ok, I could handle it, and knowing it was another lie.
    I wanted to be nothing like you.

I remember your quiet patience every time I *had* to visit.
    Each hopeful smile.
    Each glimmer of peace.
    Each pang of forgiveness seeping through.
Remembering what you had to endure.
    I wanted to forgive.

Today I remember why I wanted to be like you.
    Each tear when I leave.
    Each smile on a whim.
    Each strong stand on a belief.
I tell myself that I will be okay. I can handle it; and knowing it is true because I have forgiven you.

Peace, Love, and Stress

Darla Miller
Smyrna Middle School, Grade 7

At 7:15 Sunday evening, Trent pulled the pickup to a stop in our driveway. The three of us in the cab smelled from not having proper baths in three days, but we had stopped noticing on Friday evening. Our clothes were damp from rain, and the skies were holding yet another storm. Our bodies ached from seemingly endless walking, not to mention sleeping on clumps of grass in a cow pasture. While we were glad to be home, there was no celebration. The thrill was gone.

Being a group of eclectic music lovers, our family makes a point of attending at least one music festival each year. We use those times to reconnect with each other and escape the fast-forward mode of our routines. Trent and Rory engage in father-son chats, debating the philosophical merit of new albums. Often Trent fills Rory's head with his first-hand account of a *Van Halen* or *Rush* show. Each of us promotes our most recent musical discoveries to the others, while waiting for a band to play.

In May we attended Nashville River Stages, a three-day music festival on the Cumberland River that featured Trent's new favorite, the *Drive-By Truckers*. We all shared a double room on Music Row, drove to a parking lot, and walked to Riverfront Park each day. Trent had been looking forward to the outing as an emotional release since his job had become nearly intolerable. We heard several technically clean shows, but our musical tastes are growing, and our appetites weren't satisfied. Bonnaroo was a month away, and the artist list appealed to all of us. The plan was made. The Millers would be at Bonnaroo 2004.

Bonnaroo is an annual music festival held one weekend in June in Manchester. Since 2001, promoters have brought a host of performers that lure over 70,000 fans to a sixty-acre field leased from a local farmer. Dead Heads and college students alike fly, drive, or hitch from all over Mother Earth to be there. In only three years, it had become THE musical event of the summer. I was excited, to say the least.

With tickets in hand, my excitement transformed into concern. As I told friends and acquaintances that we were going to Bonnaroo, I heard rumors about hippies, drugs, drinking, partying, rain, mud, and general chaos at previous festivals. Believing the best preparation is education, I scoured the official website. The FAQ section proclaimed that the full experience of the festival requires camping on site. I had never gone on a camping trip before. Camping to me was a church camp where we had a cabin with a roof, a floor, a door, and a bed. The only "roughing it" was a short walk through the trees to the bathhouse. I was no longer concerned. I was worried.

As I continued perusing the site, worry morphed into outright panic at the words, "no electricity," and "no showers." I immediately planned to rent an RV. My husband chuckled and assured me that my fears were misplaced. He promised we would all survive, and he reasoned that we would be so busy at the concerts and other activities, we wouldn't be at camp long enough for problems. He even helped pick out a tent at Wal-Mart. As I read message boards from previous Bonnaroosters, as they prefer to be called, I compared lists of what others were taking. Worry subsided to concern.

I set about the business of preparing for the trip. Being fair-skinned, I knew the one item that was an absolute necessity was sun block, preferably with an SPF of 5000. I returned to Wal-Mart and Big Lots three times where I snagged bottled water by the case, and invested in a five-day cooler. Other recommended items went into the shopping cart: toilet paper, baby wipes, towels, flashlights, extra batteries, spray bottles, personal fans, more bottled water. As I gathered items, my worry resurfaced.

Our kitchen began to resemble moving day at a college dorm. When I finished, the bed of the truck held three coolers, one monstrous suitcase, two fifteen-gallon tubs, a 10x12 tent, 10x10 canopy, twelve bungee cords, one guitar case, three sling chairs, a card table, and a laundry basket with extra tent stakes, a solar light, flagpole, and camping lantern. Deciding to skip campsite cooking, we opted to eat from the vendor stands in Centeroo, the venue area. As I packed, my brain kicked into overdrive. How far we would have to walk to use the restroom, get food, get extra ice, and see the shows? What if the food prices were too high? What if we ran out of money? What if I forgot something we really needed? Would Trent and Rory have to miss events they wanted to see because I was too hot, too tired, or too manic? Anxiety arose within me.

The concerts didn't begin until 12:30 on Friday, but the gates were scheduled to open at 8:00 am Thursday. Trent had to work, so we planned to leave when he got home. I slept late hoping my fears would stay in my pillows—PILLOWS?! We'll need them to sleep on! My mind screamed, "What else have I forgotten?" Panic set in, and it paralyzed me for hours. Packing wasn't an option because I feared finding problems with what was already packed. When Trent's car sounded on the gravel outside, I didn't even have clothes in the suitcase!

The door opened, and the man I love—the man who had spent the last six months miserable at work, frustrated with his job, dissatisfied with the housework, and generally unhappy—this man bounded in the door and shouted, "Bonnarooooooooooooooooooooooo!" As he grabbed me, and I returned his hug, I sighed, and exhaled every last molecule of concern, worry, and anxiety. I inhaled the scent of his cologne, and it smelled of excitement, anticipation, and joy.

Summertime at Grandma's House

Stacy Ryel
Smyrna High School, Grade 9

I remember barefoot expeditions on hot pavement searching for our glass treasures. Discarded pop bottles found on the side of the road could bring five cents apiece if in good condition.

I remember the feeling of the cool metal as the coin met my hot hand, the reward for burnt and skinned up toes. On a good day we could pocket fifty cents, but usually we spent it all on candy or ICEEs before leaving the corner convenience store, both of which would melt the moment we walked out the door.

I remember sweltering Sunday afternoon trips to the "jewelry store" – grandpa's version of a treasure hunt. We piled into the dingy bed of grandpa's old green pickup to search the dumpsters behind a busy strip mall, sifting through discarded merchandise from the retailers, hoping to claim a treasure. Sometimes our booty was worthless, but occasionally we hit the mother load: old sticky nail polish, vases chipped but not broken, or a piece of jewelry that was slightly bent or tarnished. It was always a treat to "shop" with grandpa.

I remember the sound of the heavy screen door at the back of grandma's little brick house. Squeeeeak-CLAP! Squeeeeak – CLAP! That crotchety door scolded us as we ran in and out of her. Sometimes the squeeeeak – CLAP was followed by wails of pain as the worn-out, angry door claimed little fingers that had failed to move in time to avoid her snapping jaws.

I remember the games of children, imaginations ignited by grandpa's countless ghost stories. Dipping below the horizon, the golden orb of daylight invited a whispered dare, a sprint through the crumbling old graveyard, lungs bursting with the weight of the only breath we had dared to breathe before our mad dash; then laughter and sighs of relief on the other side of the fence as the last cousin tumbled over the fence, as the sun slipped away.

I remember catching fireflies at dusk and turning their glowing abdomens into psychedelic war paint by squishing them between our grimy fingers and smearing the iridescent goo on our faces. We would chase one another then, shooting pop bottle rockets at our opponents, only to feel the sting of grandma's flyswatter on the back of our legs when she caught us. Homemade ice cream soothed our parched throats, and a cool evening breeze arrested the cruel Oklahoma heat, if only for a moment.

I remember sitting in a darkened room, plush bed pallets stealing all available floor space, a window air conditioner rasping in the background. Stinky sweat and dirt had been scrubbed from our bodies, bodies now clad in grandpa's soft, clean undershirts that smelled of Borax and Clorox. We settle in to watch "Gunsmoke" with grandpa on his rabbit-eared television set – Festus was his favorite character, so he became ours as well. Grandma always delivered some kind of late night treat – maybe popcorn, or cheese toast, or chocolate ice cream.

I remember the piercing odor of Vick's Vapo-Rub wrestling with the scents of Ben Gay and Hall's mentho-lyptus cough drops as grandma and grandpa performed their evening "getting ready for bed" routine. The water ran in the bathroom as they tucked their teeth away for the night, then "click." and the light went out. A soft, "Goodnight, you kids," from grandma meant no foolin around, but whispers in the dark and giggles under the covers inevitably brought an "If I have to come in there…" admonition from behind the closed door. Crickets and dogs exchanged salutations. Finally, only the sound of sleeping children worn out from a day at grandma's house.

Glimpses...

Paige Hawkins
LaVergne Middle School, Grade 7

I remember the aroma of fried bologna while staying with my Papa...
...I remember the inevitable call my mother received about Papa's cancer.

I remember performing the most fantastic plays with my sisters...
...I remember my parents watching lovingly and proudly.

I remember the feel of the crisp, black habit belonging to Sister Joseph Mary as she bent down to offer me an encouraging hug...
...I remember the reason I became a teacher.

I remember the enormous, white slopes of snow that we tackled as children...
...I remember the hollow, cold feel of the igloo my father built just for us.

I remember a waking to the sounds of Bob Dylan in the early mornings of my childhood...
...I remember groaning-"Here we go again!"

I remember middle of the night journeys to Florida with my family...
...I remember sunburned shoulders and grainy PB&Js on the beach.

I remember slumber parties full of daring pranks and girlish laughter...
...I remember the exhausted feeling the very next day.

I remember the boys I "loved"...
...I remember the boys who broke my adolescent heart.

I remember the friendships I enjoyed in high school....
...I remember those that lasted and those that drifted away.

I remember my first week in college...
...I remember my Dad hovering over his little girl with great anxiety.

I remember meeting my husband in college...
...I remember feeling spontaneous, instant love.

I remember my rainy wedding day...
...I remember the feeling of everlasting love.

I remember my first teaching job…
…I remember thinking a week later I had made a big mistake.

I remember the first child who confessed I was a cool teacher…
…I remember feeling the love I felt for teaching all over again.

I remember our first child- a puppy- tiny, furry, and full of spunk…
…I remember the moment knowing I would always have a loving companion in my life.

I remember overwhelming jubilation when I learned I was expecting my first baby…
…I remember the sadness when it was taken away a week later.

I remember the day my son was born…
…I remember thinking, "What have I done?" on many sleepless nights.

I remember my son's first smile…
…I remember knowing why I ventured into parenthood.

I remember the birth of my precious little girl twenty-one months later…
…I remember my son exclaiming, "This is my sissy!"

I remember so many spectacular snapshots ..
…I remember- still.

The Hole in the Screen

Diane Kelley
Wilson Eementary School, Grade 3

I remember many many years ago visiting at my grandparents' home in Christiana, Tennessee. After church services at Millersburg Baptist Church, we would go to my grandparents for lunch on Sundays. There was one particular Sunday I remember very well.

After devouring a scrumptuous meal my grandmother had prepared, we settled down for a nap. My grandmother, Aunt Ree, and I had chosen to sleep on the cool hardwood floor since the house was not air conditioned. My mother and grandfather were not tired and chose to sit and talk in rockers on the back porch.

As we were lying on the bedroom floor, I turned on my right side facing the living room. While I lay there, I realized there was a hole in the window screen. As I continued to stare, something began crawling through the hole in the ancient screen. Much to my surprise it was a six-foot chicken snake. The long dark spotted snake crawled under a chest of drawers which was about eighteen inches extended from the floor with four tall legs. This area was so dark that it looked as though the snake was trying to locate a hiding place.

At first, I was so overwhelmed with excitement that I could not get up from the floor. Grandmother and Aunt Ree were sound asleep so I chose to tell Granddaddy and Momma about the creepy creature. I said, "Momma, there's a snake in the living room." Momma could not believe the story I was telling. She said, "Diane, it couldn't be a snake!" I pleaded with her to come and look. She did and after seeing the horrid reptile, she said, "It sure is a snake!" My grandfather got a garden hoe, dragged it out from under its secret hideaway, laid it in the fresh mowed grass, and proceeded to kill the chicken snake.

After that excitement on Sunday afternoon, the window screen had to be repaired. That was the end of sleeping on the floor and I felt like a hero.

Cooper Reed

Kelli Sims
Rock Springs Elementary School, Grade 5

I remember the sterile smell as the sleek glass doors slowly slid open.
I remember the lengthy painful walk to the room that would become your first sight.
I remember the swift steady thumping beat of the monitor that measured your hearts rhythm.
That was the day the Lord blessed me with you.

I remember watching the hands of the clock move at a sluggish pace as the hours passed awaiting your appearance.
I remember the fear of anticipation as my family left and our uncertain journey began.
I remember the jostling and noisy clanking as the nurses prepared for your arrival.
That was the day the Lord blessed me with you.

I remember the silence that seemed to fill all of eternity as I awaited your first gasp of air.
I remember my eyes became engulfed with tearful emotion as I saw your precious feet.
I remember the swelling of my heart as you were placed in my arms and our eyes connected.
That was the day the Lord blessed me with you.

I remember the hours that raced through the day as I studied your every breath.
I remember the exhausting sound of your midnight cries, which awakened me with a feeling of reassurance.
I remember the day you turned to me for comfort and protection, proving your understanding of my love for you.
I thank the Lord everyday for blessing me with you.

Tobacco Kisses

April Sneed
Rock Springs Middle School, Grade 7

I remember the aroma of musty silk flowers and chicken-n-dumplins and steam rising from the stove, heating the small space to its boiling point.

And the frail, bent frame of my great grandmother, Mamie, whose deep wrinkles told her life's story without the raspy voice even uttering a sound.

And now, with time and generations apart, reflecting on one similarity we share: growing old before our time.

I remember the small glass bowl constantly replenished with M & M's resting on the wobbling table, enticing tiny fingers to visit.

And those fingers leaving, stained brown, red, green.

I remember the tin box trailer, not quite big enough for me to lay down sideways.

And the wet, Kentucky tobacco kisses on my cheek that made me cringe so as a child.

I vividly remember the sultry summer visits to her cozy tin box, wishing with a longing now to return to those simple moments just once more.

And wanting desperately for Mamie to know then how fondly the memories of the brief time I shared with her would be to me as an adult.

Stress Relief

Marsha Blackmon
Cedar Grove Elementary School, Grade 2

There we stood, three teachers, anxiously waiting in line, our big day finally here. We had driven the night before, eaten a nice dinner, and gone to bed early in preparation for our upcoming journey. Of course, the giggling and hushed whispers had carried on late into the night, but we were still up and raring to go bright and early.

It was an overcast day, and the crowd was minimal. We could hardly wait to get through the gates, wind around all the metals posts, and push through the turnstile. Finally, we were right there, listening to the screams, feeling the wind gushing by, and hearing the screech of the brakes as the car came to a grinding halt in front of us. We excitedly boarded our first roller coaster ride at Kentucky Kingdom, feeling like little kids discovering the freedom of youth.

We buckled our belts tightly, pulled down our shoulder harnesses, gripped the pads until our knuckles turned white, and off we went. Up, up, up we climbed, the anxiety building as we went. Suddenly, the rush of the freefall pushed our stomachs up into our throats! We were screaming and laughing as we catapulted around curves, up hills, over bumps, and even upside down. Two or three minutes later, the ride ended abruptly, our necks jerked back against the headrest, and our stomachs caught up with us a few seconds later. Laughter and expressions of fun flowed from us as we exited the cart and descended the ramp.

Over and over, all day long, we ran from one coaster to another coaster to another. As the day wound down, we grudgingly exited our last ride and hiked back to the car. As we poured our tired, exhilarated selves back into the car for the trip home, the sense of freedom, fun, and reckless abandon would travel with us back home giving us memories to cherish and excited anticipation of trips to come.

The New Girl

Rebecca Foster
Buchanan Elementary School, Grade 2

The bell rang. Excitement buzzed throughout the room as we scurried to our seats all ready and set for the first day of the fourth grade. I surveyed the room, making a swift approach to size up the rest of the class. How grown up we were, now that we were in the upper grades of elementary school. Everyone was excited to see familiar faces as we exchanged enchanting stories from the summer we had grown to love. I glanced across the aisle in time to see a new face sitting silently, examining her recently sharpened pencils. She was dressed in pink shorts and a crisp striped blouse: her dark face framed with braided hair. I thought to myself what a pretty little girl she was: all neat and well-trimmed. She was the most perfect picture of a fourth grader there ever was, not to mention a future new friend in my mind. I finally caught her eye in time to flash a charming "wanna be friends?" smile. Excitement welled up in me as I waited with anticipation for a similar response. She paused for a moment, browsed through her desk to make sure all was in order, and then turned the other way. I was quite perplexed and did not know what to do. After all, had I not just shown her my friend-winning smile? Perhaps she didn't see me. After mustering the courage to try a second time, our eyes met again, and I said, "Hi. What school did you come from?" I was shocked when I realized she was sticking her tongue out at me! Then, as soon as the teacher's back was turned, I found her foot swinging across the aisle and kicking my leg.

So, from then on "day in, day out" it was war. She would kick, pinch, punch, or pull at any given moment of the day. I, in turn, would often respond in the same manner, or even seek the opportunity to be the official class name-taker. I found joy in writing her name on the board along with a checkmark for each time she looked my way. And so it was throughout my fourth grade career.

ELEVEN YEARS LATER:

Laughter spread through my group of friends as we lost ourselves in light-hearted conversation, while the mist from a man-made waterfall tickled our noses. I was in a perfectly content state until She came into view. I had not seen her since that dreaded year of rivalry, but people like her don't quickly escape your mind. I recognized her immediately as she horned in on my territory to talk to one of *my friends*, who knew her in high school. I sat silently, waiting for her to notice me, until I realized the conversation was over, and she was about to walk away. Half relieved and half disappointed, I looked at her one last time. Not knowing what to expect, our eyes met. She had a puzzled look on her face as she said, "Don't I know you?" I flashed her a dazzling smile and said that I thought we had been in school together. Then, it happened. I saw the light bulb flick on in her mind, and she said, "You're Becca Gibbs, aren't you?! Oh girl, I was so mean to you in school. You were so much taller than me, and I thought for sure you would beat me up!"

HERDSTART

Vickie Rohloff
Roy Waldron School, Grade 5

I sat drinking a steaming cup of coffee, eyes half-closed, brain not yet in gear, trying to open the window of my mind on that pre-dawn fall morning. The quiet was shattered suddenly by the baying of our hounds, and unfamiliar sounds from the back porch startled my sleepy mind into alertness. As I slowly opened the door I wondered what creature had found its way into the yard. A raccoon? A skunk? An opossum? As I stood peering into the semi-darkness, shapes became sharper outlines. The two hounds were bouncing back and forth, their baying becoming indignant as the creature ignored them.

I could make out something just a few feet away – something about waist-high and moving uncertainly. Keeping my eyes on the creature, I groped behind me for the porch light. Golden light flooded the porch and carport. A goat? A goat! What was a goat doing on my porch? To whom did it belong?

A faded brown collar encircled its neck. It was brown and white with long horns growing back and outward. Its hooves shifted quietly on the concrete and its tail twitched in anticipation. Its long scraggly beard caught the breeze, and the distinctive odor of billy goat shrouded the porch like an invisible veil. My gasp of surprise was returned with an inquisitive stare. Laughter erupted from me at such an unexpected sight.

The hounds had ceased their baying and were now sniffing and exploring the billy as he stood patiently looking at me. He didn't bolt away as I neared him, but backed off a few feet, turned his head, and began to walk around the carport inspecting the tools, the lawnmower, and automotive supplies. "Well, I'll just let you do your thing," I said unsurely, not really knowing what exactly that was.

He was still prowling about the yard when I left for school. I gave him no further thought as I immersed myself in the day's lessons. Reading, writing, English, and spelling, grading papers, attending a faculty meeting, and then a grade-level conference kept my mind occupied. The long drive home brought reflections of the school day.

As I pulled into the driveway, I remembered the billy goat. I saw no sign of him grazing in the yard. My eyes suddenly caught a movement on the front porch. The hounds were rising to greet me – as was the billy goat. As I stopped the truck, the two hounds and the goat, all bounded off the porch and came up to the truck to greet me. I laughingly told each hello and paused to look closer at the goat. Definitely a billy, I didn't need eyes to tell me that! As I walked to the back door, he trailed after me and followed me into the house.

"Oh, no!" I exclaimed. "You aren't coming in here." I shooed him out the door and closed it firmly. A few minutes later I looked out the back window and saw him standing on the lounge chair in the back yard. He was happily walking back and forth using it much like a seesaw. The beagle and the basset watched him for a few seconds then wandered off to do their hound exploring. After several minutes of seesawing, he stretched out in the lounge chair bathed in the shade of the surrounding hackberry trees.

By the time my husband returned from work, the goat was back on the front porch with the hounds. Their greeting to him was an echo of the greeting they had given me. My husband snapped a leash to his collar, and we spent the evening walking up and down the road looking for "Billy's" owner. This was not a quick chore as Billy stopped to feed on choice honeysuckle and dried thistles. The beagle and basset trailed along on our evening stroll, and passersby waved and smiled. We found Billy's owner after two stops. The man was quite frustrated with the goat and offered to sell him for twenty dollars. It seemed like a bargain at the time.

Over the next few weeks, we cleaned out the barn, cleared the fencerows, and put up $4500 of new woven wire fence. Yes, Billy was turning out to be quite a bargain. What was Billy doing during these weeks of labor? He continued to hang out on the porch with the hounds, ran cars with them, paraded up and down the road in search of choice weeds, helped with our yard work, surprised the meter reader, ate my grapevine wreath, stood and watched the linemen repair electrical lines, scared the UPS man, and generally created quite a stir when many people slowed down for a second look at that goat on the porch.

Billy grew by leaps and bounds when he discovered the dog chow. He became increasingly active, and, as a result, we bought him a few girlfriends to keep him occupied. The nanny goats kidded the following spring, and the tiny herd began to grow.

Over the years we have upgraded our herd, and Billy was eventually replaced. However, I'll never forget the old boy that started our journey of raising goats, and the many chuckles he gave us still bring a smile of remembrance.

Oh, Boy!

D'ann Cooper
Smyrna Elementary School, Grade 5

The ultimate dream for some girls is to get married and have children. My dream began to come true on December 19, 1987, my wedding day.

In November of 1989, after much pleading and discussing, my husband, Terry finally gave in. As usual, he felt financing could possibly be an issue. After convincing him that children were never going to get any cheaper, we decided to begin our family.

It wasn't long before I began having "signs" of being you know what! We were amazed it could have happened so quickly. Terry and I waited a while longer, enjoying our denial that I might be over reacting or imagining things. Finally, I made a doctor's appointment to secure our peace of mind. On January 2, 1990, I took a pregnancy test. It was positive; what a way to start off the new year!

The two of us were really excited; Terry's reaction was perhaps a little more tinged with shock! Our families were happy for us, too. They knew I wanted a baby, but had no idea we were considering it at that time.

I really wanted a girl. All I could think of was dressing her in pink, frilly dresses (my mom loves to sew), lacy panties and bows in her hair! It didn't matter to "Daddy" what "it" was; he was determined to spoil "it" no matter what.

Terry and I weren't sure if we wanted to learn our baby's sex ahead of time, but we did want to be prepared before "it" arrived. In May, when I had my ultrasound, Terry and I could no longer stand the suspense. Both of us gave in and we decided to find out! The nurse jiggled my belly to get the baby to move around. On the small, five inch screen, I couldn't tell what anything was. The main purpose of the ultrasound was to be sure that the baby was developing properly. We were relieved to know everything was proceeding normally. Now it was time to find out if "it" was a girl or boy. The nurse jiggled my stomach some more and said, "It's a girl; I don't see anything hanging between her legs." I asked her to please look again to make sure. I convinced myself she had to be right because she did this for a living. She looked again, and again she said, "I'm pretty sure it's a girl."

"Wow, that's great! I guess all those pink, strawberry milkshakes paid off," I said to myself. I was so excited, I couldn't wait to tell everyone. With another female coming into the house, all Terry could think about was the checking account staying in the red!

Friends gave us a baby shower in June. We received an abundance of pink—dresses, ruffly outfits, bows, shoes and everything else we needed for our baby girl. We decorated her room to go either way however, because we wanted to be able to use it for our next baby as well.

My due date was approaching very quickly. Our baby, Jessica Leeanne, was due on Monday, August 13, 1990. Both of my parents were teachers at the time and they were starting school on that day. I really wanted them to be there for the birth of their granddaughter. My doctor, not aware of this, gave us the option of inducing labor on Friday the tenth, or waiting until labor began on its own. Saturday the eleventh was my birthday and I knew the chances of her being born on that day were very slim. Terry and I decided to go for the tenth knowing that we would not get to make the unexpected, frantic run to the hospital in the middle of the night!

I went to the hospital on Friday morning around 7:30, and was hooked up and ready to start labor by 9:15 A.M. I just knew this day was going to last forever. Food, of course, was forbidden to me. I'll never forget the torture my dad put me through by eating Peanut M & M's in my birthing room—they are my very favorite. Other than that, everything went well during labor. The closer I came to delivery, the more nervous and excited we became. Terry and I were anxiously awaiting the arrival of Jessica Leeanne. We had chosen the name Jessica just because we liked it. Leeanne was a combination of names from Mommy, Daddy, and both grandmothers. She was a very beloved child already and she wasn't even here yet.

I was getting really close to delivering around 4:40 P.M. The doctor was called at this time. I realized the nurse was getting a little antsy waiting on the doctor to arrive. I wasn't sure she thought he would make it to me in time! The nurse stood there with her hand on little Jessica's head, delaying her arrival in my eager arms.

As soon as the doctor arrived and washed up, it was show time! I was ready to push. I pushed and pushed until I thought my head was going to blow off and suddenly, at 5:25 P.M. out popped Jessica. Or so we thought. The doctor proclaimed, "Little Boy!" Oh boy, was I in shock or what? I didn't know whether to laugh or cry. All I could think of was all the pink we had. I didn't think our little boy would look too masculine in a pink, frilly dress. I lay there thankful that he was a perfect baby. Once past the surprise, we inquired if our new baby was all right. Indeed he was; Jessica had all her parts, plus one!

The hardest part was telling everyone when they came in to see us, that she was a he. The looks on their faces were priceless. I don't think anyone believed us until they saw proof for themselves.

Fortunately, we had a boy's name picked out also. We named our bouncing baby boy Robert Joseph after both of his grandfathers. He has been a joy to them and the whole family for all the years we've had him, almost fourteen of them now. We would not trade him for a million screaming, squealy girls. He is an awesome son, a fine young man, a gifted athlete, and we are very proud of him and his younger brother, Spencer, whom we "knew" was going to be a boy!

A Rude Awakening

Monte Parks
Rock Spring Elementary School, Grade 5

Whatever happened to the fly in buttermilk? I was once that fly. I had never experienced something quite like this; however, it opened my eyes to the sometimes sad, but often present, condition of life.

Having grown up on military bases, I never really noticed the differences in people. I knew that some people have straight, light hair; some have wavy, dark hair; and some have kinky, pitch hair. Then there are those who have creamy pale skin, sun-bronzed skin, or a dark chocolate tone. I knew that people were different, but I did not realize that it mattered. I had never made this connection, nor had I ever been asked to do so.

I was so excited about starting kindergarten in 1985. I woke up excited and skipped off to a new world of learning. I met new people and made many new friends. Everything was wonderful. What a new world it turned out to be!

About two or three weeks into the school year, the class was going out to recess and I was just as excited this day as I had been any other day. I was going to have a chance to play with my new friend. Just as recess was starting, I was introduced to something very ugly. My friend told me that she was not allowed to play with black people. As I sat on the jungle gym alone, many thoughts began to play through my young mind.

First, if she was not supposed to play with me, why had we played together before? This was the very first time that I had ever actually been aware of the fact that I seemed different in a negative way. I understood that God had made us all different and I was always taught that it was not a bad thing to be any race. I knew I looked different, in fact I was the only black student in my class, but I never knew that it mattered. There I sat all alone.

I was not alone for long because another group of my friends came by and I began to play with them. I had just as much fun, and I did not have to worry about my appearance with this group of friends. They proved to be real friends. I played with them every day for the rest of kindergarten and even into later grades in elementary school. There were times that I was placed on the same team or in the same group as the girl, but we never really played together again.

Later, I realized that the incident was brought on by a snap-bead necklace I would not give this so-called-friend. But still, it was a difficult situation for me. I must admit I learned a lot of positive things from a bad situation. First, I learned that often times, people make mistakes due to ignorance. To this day, when I see this person, she is overly nice. I would even say that she is apologetic. I also learned that everyone I meet in life is not my friend, but I still must treat him or her fairly and with respect. I thank God for this experience because it helped shape me into the person I am. Hopefully it also helped that girl as well. I never held any hard feeling toward her, but I can honestly say I will never forget.

EEEE Gads!

Nancy S. Peterman
Rock Springs Elementary School, Grade 3

One summer we had gone to Grandpa's house for a visit. I loved to go there because he lived in a big two-story house way out in the country with a pecan orchard as part of his property. There were several places to have an adventure, from roaming through the many rooms in the house to exploring the family cemetery.

On this particular day, Mom had decided I had had enough adventure and needed to take a rest. We lay down on Grandpa's bed, but both of us were having difficulty going to sleep. We had a sensation of something moving beneath us, and this was not normal with an old cotton mattress. Finally, my mother decided to investigate. She rolled back the old yellowed mattress, such as one would see on the bunks in a church camp, to reveal a snake. It was coiled up in the middle of the box springs and had been sandwiched between the mattresses. Seeing this sight and knowing that we had just been laying on top of that very mattress sent us into a screaming fit that would have raised the dead. Grandpa came on the double to see what the ruckus was about only to quickly retreat and return with a sledgehammer. I remember watching him use the sledgehammer, and it seemed he hit every spot on the bed but where the snake was. My mother and Grandpa changed places. Since Mom's eyesight was better, she quickly nailed her target. My last visual impression of the black snake with diamonds down its back was seeing it draped over a garden rake as it was being carried out of the house.

One might wonder: how did the snake get into the house in the first place? So did we. The only solution that we could arrive at was that he came in through the floor where one of the slats in the hard wood flooring had popped out of its place leaving a snake-sized opening.

Needless to say, we didn't take a nap that day. I had never liked to take a nap, but that was not how I wanted to avoid one ever again!

Letter to My Best Friend

Vicki Petty
Central Middle School, Grade 8

Dear Sally,

Has it really been over four years since you left this earth? So many times after you were gone, I found myself reaching for the phone to call you. Your number stayed on my speed dial for a year. I could not bring myself to delete your name even though you could never be deleted from my mind. I think of you often, but lately you have been in my thoughts more than ever.

This is the summer of the class reunion for our Central High School Class of 1969. I found myself looking through the yearbook and found your letter to me with pictures of our high school days. Looking at that picture of two young ladies from different backgrounds, yet best friends, flooded me with so many wonderful memories! We were headed for different places and different experiences, but our friendship would endure.

Did you know that our class established a scholarship. And that many donations have been made in your memory? Those that attended the reunion remembered those who had been lost over the last thirty-five years. I know you would never believe that you were admired and loved by so many and are remembered fondly. I knew you well enough to know that you would not care one way or another, as you always did it your way. You knew me well enough to know that I do care.

There was never any doubt that we would remain close friends after graduation. You were a bridesmaid in my wedding and the godmother of my first-born son . You did not think that you would ever find a husband, but I knew there was someone very special who would love and cherish you. Later you married, and in that same year lost your beautiful mother. I shared your joy and sadness that year.

You moved away with your new husband and had your three children. We exchanged birthday and Christmas cards with a few phone calls in between. We did not see each other very often as we were so busy with life. We made plans to get together soon; there was plenty of time. Next year we would meet for lunch and catch up.

The news of your breast cancer hit me like a ton of bricks. This could not be true! You had always taken such good care of yourself. You ate healthy and exercised. You took all precautions and treatments, and I was certain this would be okay. You were so positive for so long that this could not get you down.

You tried every available treatment known in modern medicine and we thought the terrible monster disease would disappear. You did not talk to many people, including family. You never failed to answer my phone calls, however, and I always felt that you were trying harder to cheer me. You wanted to hear about my life and family rather than talk about your illness.

After four years of fighting this battle, your sister gave me the call I never wanted to receive. I felt as if a part of me had died. I felt guilty that I had not been with you in those last months. I should have called you more, I should have visited you more, and why didn't I make that time? I cried for your husband, your three beautiful children, your father and siblings, and for the friends like me that would miss your beauty and grace. I cried for the grandchildren you would not spoil. I cried for myself and the best friend that I had lost.

I survived the guilt. I know that you knew how much our friendship meant to me. I started telling my other friends how special they are. I make those phone calls and visits for your sake. I encourage others to cherish friends, sharing the good and the bad. Most of all, Sally, I am writing to thank you for touching my life.

Your best friend,
Vicki

Silence is Golden

Sunita Watson
Barfield Elementary School, Grade 2

I noticed a bird. I think it was a crane. Yes, it was a white crane printed on a navy flight bag. My life began on that airplane.

As a two year-old baby, I remember the smell of being on the Japanese Airline flight from Calcutta to the United States. It was a curry-ish odor, but not the kind I was used to. It hung in the air and clung to my shirt and my skin. Everything was yellow—the light, the walls, the whole ambiance—even the smell was yellow like curry powder. I can't remember seeing my mother or father but I recall the stewardess. She seemed to be a giant, but pretty, with fair skin and slanting eyes. She was nice. She talked to me, but I heard no sounds. My senses were flooded with the amber aura of the cabin bearing me toward a golden future in the land of opportunity.

Herbee's

Jonelda Buck
Smyrna Primary School, Grade 4

Absolutely nothing made me more excited on a hot, summer day than to see or hear my Grandpa Charlie's old, faded out, red pick-up truck chugging down our long, gravel, country driveway. When he came rolling down the drive anytime during the middle part of the day, I knew he was coming for one reason and one reason only. That reason being to take me to Herbee's!

Growing up a true country gal in the middle of rural Double Top Tennessee, my summers weren't spent going to the pool, watching television all day, or just hanging out with friends. My summer vacation days were spent getting up at the crack of dawn and helping my mom and dad with things that needed to be taken care of around the house and farm. Large portions of my days were spent working in our three gardens, the tobacco field, or the sweet potato patch. There was nothing I hated worse than pulling weeds from our five fields of flourishing harvest. My only saving grace from a few hours of weed pulling was for Grandpa to come and holler, "Come on Jo, let's go to Herb's." Not one time did my mom or dad ever refuse to let me climb into that old, faded, red pick-up and escape an hour or two of duties to enjoy a trip to my favorite childhood store…Herbee's.

To me, Herbee's was the absolute best treat in the world. After our anxious, fifteen minute drive to Moodyville, my grandfather and I would pull into the small parking lot. It was always interesting to see who was hanging around the store "shooting the bull" with ole' Herb. Of course, Grandpa knew them all and easily kept himself occupied by chiming in on the chatter while I pondered over what seemed like millions of possibilities of junk food that I was only allowed to get when with my Grandpa Charlie. It's important that you know that my mother never allowed her children to have junk food! If you wanted a snack, you would go warm up some green beans for yourself. Anyway, as we walked through the heavy, swinging, front door Grandpa would always say, "Alright Jo, get whatever you want." As a child, I felt like the options that this little, locally owned and operated gas station held for me choosing a few snacks were endless. After staring at the candy shelf, pacing between the drink refrigerator, the ice cream freezer, the chip stand, and con-templating the thought of maybe going for a sandwich "Herbee style" with some "sssssssslickum", that being mayonnaise, I'd finally make that big decision of what I'd get on this trip. My very own, little brown sack usually ended up carrying out a "pop", most likely a Pepsi, a candy bar, a bag of chips, and maybe one piece of three-cent bubble gum. As soon as I sat down on that old, cloth interior, truck seat my little brown poke, as my grandpa called it, opened up and I began enjoying my delicious snacks. By the time we returned to that long, gravel, country driveway, I'd usually have the first half of my brown bag contents devoured and have the other half wrapped up securely, saved for later enjoyment.

As I reflect on this favorite childhood memory and the passing of my grandpa this past February, I'm filled with such lasting thoughts of pure happiness. That once so big gas station still operates, but for some reason it's not quite so big nowadays. Mr. Herbee no longer owns the store, but the gentleman that has taken over ownership is keeping that wonderful little, one-stop shop, gas station alive with all the options of purchasing your gas, snacks, groceries, lunch, guns, ammo, knives, or rat poison all at one convenient location. You can even pick up a nice, camouflage jacket during your stop, if that's what you're looking for. I often wonder what memories my little nieces and nephews and someday my own children will cherish from their grandparents, my parents.

The Wreck on Hilton Head Island

Susan B. Cantrell
Eagleville High School, Grade 10

I am an English teacher. English teachers love literary terms. We talk about them, we bring them up in conversations, and we point them out while watching movies. Therefore, my thinking of a literary term at the time of the wreck was not an unusual event.

My husband and I went to Hilton Head Island each summer for a month. He worked on the island and I played, we lived on the golf course; we had maid service, and a convertible for me to go all over the island. The days were beautiful, restful, and full of peace.

During this month-long stay a friend of mine came up for a few days to visit. She and I worked together teaching. Our goal was to stay on the beach as long as possible each day.

We were packing up to go to the beach when she decided we should be riding bikes. Bike riding was healthier, and we would get exercise. The only problem was I could not ride a bike. I think I was born with a learning disability of not being able to balance. My friend said, "No problem, we will just get a bike built for two." She would drive and all I would have to do is help pedal. We rented the greatest two-seater bike. It was bright red with cute baskets in the front and the back. We were on our way.

The ride was going great. I thought I could do this; sort of. In order to get to the beach in Hilton Head, you have to go down one of the main streets. We were traveling along, ducking under the cypress trees, enjoying the wind on our faces. All was fine until my friend came to a place in the road where we had to turn. I was so enthralled with my ability to ride the bike; I was not paying attention to riding the bike. My friend turned but I didn't.

I remember sailing through the wind, over the handlebars of my part of the bike and then over my friend's part of the bike. It was a long descent. I landed in the street on my back, Immediately the Hilton Head police had an ambulance and were trying to see if I was alive. When I realized they were serious, I jumped up and told them I was fine and I was walking home.

I was hurt, on the inside and the outside. My legs and arms were bleeding. I had part of the street still stuck to my head and I was simply a mess. All I could think to do was get in the shower and try to get the blood and dirt off me. In the shower, was when I remembered the word I was thinking as I sailed through

102

the air, Foreshadow?

Life went on. My friend left, I healed up, and my husband finished his job and we came home. The bike wreck became a funny story and then a forgotten one.

The Hilton Head adventure was in June. Hilton Head is so beautiful in June. It is not too hot or humid and the hurricane season has not begun. Hilton Head was the calm before the storm. I was clueless to the stirrings of the spirits. Summer became difficult that year and in August my husband asked me for a divorce. His words became a time where life, breathing, seeing, thinking, ceased for a second.

The divorce was life-changing. It was a complete break in the plans for my life. There were times I did not think I would survive and times I did not want to survive. But, each year it got a little better. After several years, I began to see a new me, a new healing.

Where I live looks a lot like Hilton Head. When I first moved there, I thought of Hilton Head again. I remembered the wreck. I remembered the flying over the bike. Then I remembered the word – foreshadowing. The wreck was very much like the divorce. The foreshadowing had been a message of things to come. The metaphor for my life became the wreck. I was not paying attention to where I was going. I was interested in the glory of riding the bike. I should have been paying attention to my life, my marriage. I was hurt during the wreck but not "unto death." I was hurt terribly by the divorce but not destroyed. The inability of not paying attention when my friend turned the bike became a window to me of how little attention I had paid to so much. But, remember I jumped up off the pavement, and walked home. I rose up against my wounds. I knew I would live again and I did.

The First Kiss

Jennifer Cook
Christiana Middle School, Grade 6

Their first meeting was pitch, black darkness in the middle of the ballroom in Lester Fair, England, 1944. Both people came to the Opera House that night looking for love and little did they know this was the actual beginning of a true love affair. Her name was "Carla" and his Albert. "Carla" and her friend "Anita" both had the same name, which was Joyce. They decided since they were attending the same dance and both on the look out for a handsome service man, they should change their boring names. So, the story goes according to "Carla", she met Albert that night on the dance floor all the while surrounded by the sound of buzz bombs of WWII. Although Albert was a sailor and "Carla" preferred flyers, they decided to continue their courtship until Albert's deployment from England in 1947.

March 13, 1947, that hot and humid day in Miami was extra special for my grandparents Joyce and Albert. Not only were they now joined in matrimony, but also Albert now knew "Carla's" true identity as Joyce. I guess marriage was the only way "Carla" felt comfortable enough to confess her subterfuge. During their first nine years of marriage they welcomed three healthy children Albert, Linda, and Sandra. My mother, Linda, grew up moving from state to state, city to city, which was the common life style of a military family.

Then Linda continues the love affair by telling my brother and I that her parents Joyce and Albert always showed love, but it was a silent, kind of "secret" love. However, as a young child my eyes observed a very different love. During one of my summer vacations I spent a week at my grandparent's house. Now I wanted to see first hand what this "secret" love was all about. What I saw was extremely common of my grandparents. According to my viewpoint all they ever did was fight and bicker. My days and nights were filled with hearing my grandmother call my grandfather "Sweet Breath," "Bloody Sod," or any one of her numerous British nicknames. As a consequence, most of the time my grandfather would just roll his eyes and not say a word back to her. Now to a six-year-old little girl this seemed like a strange, but funny relationship. I would often find myself anticipating the next nasty word or spat they would have. I kind of felt like a spectator at a wrestling match cheering on one side or the other. Although, this all changed one day when we were all watching television. To the best of my recollection, they had been bickering earlier that day until . . . I got antsy. I was really hungry and wanted to eat pickles for some strange reason. My grandparents agreed they wanted some, too, and sent me into the kitchen to get some. When I returned with my jar of pickles in hand I witnessed something that is hard to explain. Although, according to this 28-year-old woman what happened next changed my entire opinion on love. As I walked into the room of all things to be doing, my grandparents were . . . KISSING. And, I don't mean just a little peck on the cheek, this was the real thing. This was a full-fledged kiss, like the ones I would see on television. I can't explain my emotions at that time. I remember being filled with mostly relief, but I also felt a mixture of happiness and awe. My grandparents were actually kissing and not fighting. "Gross," was my final thought as I smiled at them with my Cheshire cat grin. Of course, by the time they figured out that I caught them, they slowly returned to their normal kind of relationship. I think they even started squabbling just to conceal their "secret" love from me.

At this moment, looking back over the years I realize just how important that first kiss was to me. To most six-year-old children seeing a kiss is probably not such a big deal. Although to me, that kiss signified a love that I might be so lucky to find one day. My grandparents "first kiss" sealed my perception that love happens at many levels. Love is such a diverse emotion that sometimes the fighting you see on the outside is not always the same feeling of devotion on the inside. I truly thank my grandparents for etching in my heart the true meaning of love at such an early age.

"Mirror, Mirror…"

Michelle Delaney
Christiana Middle School, Grade 7

"Tell me again why I'm doing this?" I asked for what had to have been the fiftieth time since arriving at the hospital that morning. I had developed a bad case of cold-feet, frost-bitten, frigid. Only I wasn't a bride about to walk down the aisle into the arms of a waiting groom and a new life. Instead, I was about to take a gurney journey…a few hundred feet into a sterile operating room. How had I gotten here? It had taken me two years of insurance battles, NO it had taken me a lifetime, to arrive at this moment. The moment where my old life would end and a new one would take its place. I couldn't know or even imagine what lie before me. Even now as I look back on it all it still has the haze of the surreal, like the Salvidor Dali painting where everything including time seems to have melted and blurred around the edges. In that moment I knew only two things: there was no going back AND my life as I knew it was over.

"It's time," the nurse said. I handed my meager belongings to my mother who gave me the most reassuring smile she could muster under the circumstances. "I'll see you in a few hours, have a good nap," she whispered as she kissed my forehead. I could feel the slight tremor of her lips against my skin. Slowly they wheeled the gurney into the operating room where the bone-chilling cold made my teeth clitter clack. I have a vague recollection of the voices around me, a slight stinging sensation on my arm, and the nurse instructing me to count backwards from one hundred. "One hundred, ninety-nine, ninety-eight…"

"Breathe deeply," a gruff Nurse Ratchett voice ordered, "Don't be lazy!" I struggled to open my eyes, gradually becoming aware of the chills that shook me, and the pain that had settled between my shoulder blades. Strange…I thought they had stapled my stomach not hammered my shoulder blades together. Suddenly it hit me as Nurse Ratchett scolded me again about my shallow breathing; I was alive, I hadn't died on the table. The next few days passed in a morphine induced stupor with vague visions of a continuous stream of doctors, nurses, friends, family, and well-wishers.

Fast forward-fourteen months and one hundred ninety-three pounds. I was wrong I did die on that operating table, or rather, a part of me did. Or maybe I just learned how to live.

I have discovered during my arduous journey that life is very different when you weigh less than a line backer for the Raiders! It was a revelation to find in our politically correct, homogenized world of white-washed appropriateness that prejudice against the fat is not only alive and well, but thriving. The realities of what it is like to be a fat lady truly began to make themselves known as I stopped being one. In real life… fat ladies only sing and take center stage at the Opera, Fair is a word that is found often only in the dictionary, and who I thought I was isn't always who I am. I have discovered I am an Everywoman. I am in those who struggle as I have, and do, to lose those extra pounds—both the few and the many. I am in the insecurities of every beauty who cannot see herself for who she truly is. And I am, just like you, not what I was and not yet what I am going to be. I am rare, beautiful, soulful, valuable and struggling like the Velveteen Rabbit to allow myself to be loved and to love myself enough to be REAL.

Wilma, Duchess of Chadwick Drive

Lisa Gingras-Massengale
Smyrna Middle School, Grade 7

When I was seventeen, I was diagnosed with severe scoliosis. As a result, I had a spinal fusion. While my recovery was long, difficult, and painful, I had the distinct advantage of having my parents' undivided attention and sympathy. My younger sisters, fifteen and nine and used to getting their own way, watched in horror as my parents granted my every request. In one day, I received a Mickey Mouse telephone, (my sister Jessica begged for one for a year to no avail) and an Olympic Cabbage Patch Kid (my youngest sister Nikki actually cried when she found out it was for me and not her.)

After a few days of watching this, my sisters found a way to use my power for their benefit. While my parents went to get lunch at the hospital McDonald's, my sisters convinced me that I wanted a pet. (This probably wasn't too difficult given the amount of morphine pumping through my system.) They claimed to have my best interest at heart and suggested that a pet would keep me company while all of my friends were out having fun during the summer. It worked.

Although I was easily convinced, my mother would be a different story. According to her, pets were a smelly, unnecessary, time and money-consuming nuisance. Imagine her surprise (or horror) when Dad brought a small, quivering, black-nosed pet to our home on Chadwick Drive. Apparently, he picked up on the hints dropped in the hospital and brought home a piglet.

Before my mother could object, we named her Duchess Wilma and moved her into our house. The small piglet quickly grew into her name and began ruling our family. Dad taught her many tricks and after a few weeks, she could sit, stay, lie down and dance. Her reward for her performance was a piece of bacon. (We discovered her cannibalistic habit after my sister dropped a plate of bacon on the floor). My sisters and I enjoyed the quiet times with our first family pet. She loved to lie on the floor with us, usually in the small of our backs, and watch movies. Her favorite was *Babe,* and she often talked back to the screen. And when she thought no one was looking, Mom would scratch her belly and talk to her.

Even though Wilma is no longer with us, (she is currently touring elementary schools with other miniature performing farm animals), she left a lasting impression on our family. Bringing her home united three fighting sisters. Jessica and Nikki both learned about the responsibility of having a pet. Even my mother, a self-proclaimed hater of the animal world, admitted that Wilma was the smartest, cleanest, animal she ever knew and decided that maybe all animals weren't so bad. But most importantly, this little pig brought me comfort and companionship during a long, difficult, and painful summer.

My Life Began

Danette Wells
Rock Springs Elementary School, Grade 3

I was born February 14, 1971. That's what I tell people when they ask my birth date. But my life actually began the day I met you.

I thought my life was complete before you came along. I was happy. I knew who I was. I thought I had everything I needed.

After nine years of marriage, nothing I can write can truly measure up to the kind of husband you have been or the way you have completed me.

When I met you, it was a perfect time in my life for you to enter. It was spring, and I had just graduated college that past December. I was still working at the golf course, where we met. That teaching job had to be just around the corner, waiting on me. I was very content with life.

You waltzed into the golf course that spring afternoon with your brother, Dusty. Having known Dusty for a while, I could see the physical resemblance you both shared. I remember the exuberance you spewed out, taking me aback. I was so calm natured and quiet that day, like always. Being in your presence for only a few minutes, it was easy to see that you were larger than life. You left a smile on my face that remained for some time.

Lara called me later that night to ask me if I would go out with you. "How did he even notice or remember me? I was so quiet when we met. I am nothing like him. I wondered, "Why would he want to go out with me?" Lara proceeded to tell me what a great guy you were. "He has really settled down a lot lately.", she said. Since she had known you for years and worked with me, I figured she knew our personalities well enough to match us up. I said, "Yeah, that sounds like fun."

When you came to pick me up at Uncle Joe's house, you once again were larger than life, way too large for me, but you were exciting. "You would be fun to hang out with for a while", I thought. Little did I know.

Our date that night was the most fun. You weren't afraid to talk and ask questions like I normally was. Oh, no. You were hyper, funny, and bold. But I also sensed a tenderness in you that seemed so wonderful. Dinner was great. The movie, however, was awful, and I do mean awful. But it didn't matter. We talked that night with such ease and laughter. You were everything that I wasn't. I was the cautious, careful, reserved one. You were risky, out there, and in your face. But somehow, together, we seemed to balance each other. I felt really alive for the first time in my life.

When we pulled into the driveway, I knew what a great time I had had, but I didn't really know if the physical side would be there. As I looked at you sitting beside me and thanked you for the night, you leaned forward, and all reservations I had were gone. One kiss, and I knew.

Ten years and two daughters later, it's so easy to look back and see what was missing in my life before you. It was everything that your spirit possesses. You complete me, like no one else could.

When people ask my birth date, I tell them, "February 14, 1971," and then I smile to myself and think of the day I met you.

Think of Me

Kelli Sisson
Siegel High School, Grade 9

Think of me in the morning,
As you greet each brand new day,
Live life with the fullest spirit,
For me, it was the only way.

Think of me on your special day,
As you hold his hand in yours,
And pledge to love him faithfully,
I pray your love always endures.

Think of me when you laugh,
As my life was filled with joy,
Take care of him through ups and downs,
Remember, he'll always be my little boy.

Think of me when times are hard,
As I know you can make it through,
With family, friends, and Christ Jesus,
You will know just what to do.

Think of me when you pray,
As you count your blessings from above,
Have faith in God and always know,
"The greatest of these is love."

Think of me in the evening,
As you softly say goodnight,
I will forever be within your hearts,
With angel's arms around you tight.

In loving memory of Sheron Wright Nichols.

Chapter Four

Connecting through Family Memories

Who Holds My Heart

Denise Reed
Kittrell Elementary School, Grade 5

She holds my heart.
She wonders where do the colors of the rainbow go after they fade.
She hears the bird's joyous song of happiness even through the clouds.
She sees only the good in others.
She wants what is best for all dear to her.
She holds my heart.
She pretends to be strong even when she needs assistance.
She believes the love of God holds all earth's treasures.
She touches the lives of people she may only meet for a minute.
She feels the pain of those closest to her.
She worries that there isn't enough time in the day to make things right for her
family.
She weeps silently, never outwardly, carrying her own worries deep inside.
She holds my heart.
She understands me better than I understand myself.
She says what is in her heart and on her mind, always an honest answer.
She dreams of times when there will be family peace and contentment.
She hopes for a home in heaven and rest eternal from the trials of this life.
She holds my heart, my life.
She is my mother.

Connections

Lisa Ezell
Christiana Middle School, Grade 8

Curls on my daughters' heads
Ocean tides calming my soul
Never going a day without saying, "I love you."
Needing the sound of music
Eyes watching what I do
Cooking in my mother's dishes
Teaching her recipes to my children
Inching my way to personal understanding
Opening doors to my future
No intentions of retreating
Signs of myself

Blessed Mother

Ginger Adcock
Thurman Francis Arts Academy, Grade 6

I am a loved and blessed mother.

I wonder what each day holds and how my children will grow.

I believe they are sent from Heaven, a place in my heart they have to keep.

I want them to fear the Lord and of his promises know.

I pretend life is at a stand still but I know I cannot stop it; I weep.

I am a loved and blessed mother.

I hear their voices chiming, the sound of laughter coming through.

I touch their soft, warm cheeks as they lay in my arms sleeping.

I worry that I am not a good mother yet promise to be understanding and say, "I love you".

I see them before my eyes as ever changing.

I feel more love than I deserve, but of his plan God knew.

I cry as each phase ends and I pack up all of their out-grown things to make room for a new beginning.

I am a loved and blessed mother.

I understand that no matter how old they are they will forever be mine.

I say a thankful prayer each night that I am their mother to the Lord above.

I dream that they will be happy and perpetually shine.

I hope the world treats them kindly and they always know of love.

I am a loved and blessed mother.

Grandaddy

Faith Burgess
Christiana Elementary School, Kindergarten

His cars and trucks were so worn out that I didn't think they would make it to the farm one more time. As soon as I would see the duct tape, I knew he had an ingenious plan. It always worked.

His pants are worn out and just a little tight around the waist. I'm sure that his socks don't match, that is not important. His boots are over 30 years old. The shirt he wears is probably most definitely stained with grease and bleach, just like his pants. It is hard to work on machinery and not get dirty. Some of the buttons on his shirt barely meet and are pulled together. But, it is not too small because it still buttons. His glasses are big and brown. I am sure they are old, but they still work. It would be wasteful to buy something new, like glasses when the old ones still work fine.

He said we should save our money. You just don't need a lot of anything. Sam and Michael and I are being wasteful when we buy lots of shoes. You only need one pair, and maybe one more pair for church. His boots lasted 31 years!! He told Michael, "They just don't make them like they used to." He called my house a big bungalow. It was just too big for two people. All Michael and I needed was a bedroom, bathroom and kitchen, maybe a den with a TV. He thought it was so important that you know what was going on in the world and especially what Bush said.

What ever happened to the handshake? We would go to the car lot and buy the oldest and cheapest car on the lot. After he shook hands with the salesman, he'd ask, "Is this guaranteed?" "Oh yes sir, Mr. Hardin." He would get so mad that he didn't even speak when he would go back soon there after and he would have to pay for repairs. All he would say is "highway robbery."

I remember sitting on the tailgate of his truck and eating watermelon still warm from the field. He always put salt on his piece, I didn't like mine that way. He would sometimes cut it with his dirty pocket-knife. Who knows where that knife had been. He considers it sanitary after he wipes it on his pants one good time.

I remember going over to his house when I was little and him grabbing my hand as soon as I walked inside. He would hold it tight and not let it go. That was his way of saying I love you.

You can always find him sitting in his big old leathery, vinyl recliner watching TV or reading. He doesn't read for fun, he reads for knowledge. On Wednesday and Friday, you can catch him reading the Wayne County News and The Hardin County paper cover-to-cover, careful not to miss the obituaries. When you are 92 years old, you usually know someone each week who has died. If you want to know about politics, he can tell you that too. His opinion is strong. When he isn't reading, he is watching the news or CSPAN. That is where he gets all his information.

When I was in college, I would hurry to show him my grades. He never said a thing. We knew he was proud. He expected nothing but good grades. But, he wouldn't have said anything if they were bad. He was so proud of Sam and me when we graduated and got married, but he never said a thing. We could just tell.

I married Michael, and from the first time he met Grandaddy, I knew he loved him and respected him. He talks about him all the time just like he is his grandfather, too. Grandaddy treats him just like he treats us. That's why I can threaten to tell granddaddy when I think that Michael "messes up." You know that if you ever hear "What seems to be the problem?" that something is about to happen. You are probably going to hear what you should do, in his opinion, to solve that problem.

I love hearing my niece Lexie beg to go over to Grandaddy's house. She can't wait to see the puppies or kittens. He always takes care of animals, especially ones with out moms. You should see him feed a one-week old kitten with a medicine dropper. As soon as the kittens are ready to go live independently at the farm, be assured that something else will need his care and attention. He will grumble about all the cats or all the dogs, but I think inside he loves helping them. Lexie loves to watch her great-grandfather play with the kitties.

He never judged Sam, Michael, and me when we would make HUGE mistakes. He helped by just not saying anything. I think that was the most effective method. I was thinking, "What's he thinking?" He was probably thinking that we would learn from our mistakes and that was a lesson.

I just liked the feeling that I got when I knew he was proud of me. I know that he is proud. I have a college degree, a wonderful husband, and a nice house. I am independent; he is proud.

Most of all, I love the feeling I get when I come home after being away for awhile. Michael and I are so glad to see him that we go straight there. We don't want to get to Clifton late or he will already be in bed when we get there. He grins so big, that I know he is excited to see us. We could sit and talk for hours unaware of the time. It just feels so good.

He is hard-headed. It is his way or no way. And, after 92 years of living and working very hard, his way is usually the right way.

By saying nothing all those times, he has said so much. I will always remember that.

Grief

Kay Starrett
Riverdale High School, Grades 9 and 11

I am sad, grieving, alone.
I wonder why we ever have to experience loss.
I hear her laughter, her jokes, her songs.
I see her smiles, her love, her legacy.
I want her back.

I am sad, grieving, alone.
I pretend that I'm okay.
I believe that she is at peace and life should go on as usual.
I touch her hands, her hair, her scars.
I feel a sense of loneliness I cannot describe.
I worry that my children won't remember her.
I cry at night so no one will know.

I am sad, grieving, alone.
I understand that death is simply a part of living.
I dream she is still with me.
I hope that we will once again be together when Christ reunites our souls.
But for now…
I am sad, grieving, alone.

My Boys: Caleb and Parker

Dawn Powell
Christiana Middle School, Grade 6

Brothers:
Apart by two years,
but same size they appear.
No memories of a time, when the other wasn't there,
Having only each other, with nothing to compare.

Best friends:
Sorting stuffed animals, building tents, playing spies;
Comforting his buddy, whenever he cries.
Annoying each other, pressing buttons towards a fight;
Dad brings out the gloves, and then they unite.

First born:
Self motivated, and striving for perfection,
Defending all creatures, who need his protection.
Eyes of blue, and a vulnerable spot,
Compassion for all, who deserve it or not.

Baby boy:
With the need to touch ears, and carefree ambition,
Showing no fear, seeking Bru Bru's permission.
Big blue eyes, pay attention to see,
the way to DRIVE IT, and DIG IT; always busy, but worry-free.

God knew what he was doing,
the way he answered my prayers.
Those daughters, I yearned for,
could never compare...

To the joy my sons give me,
when they hold each other tight.
Or when they pray for each other,
at bedtime each night.

Mandy

Missy Smigielski
John Colemon Elementary School, Grade 4

Amanda Joyce the glue of the clan
always takes matters into hand.

High-spirited, dedicated, and driven
was to us God-given.

She strikes like a bolt of lightning
which to us is kind of frightening.

Her beliefs are strong when asked to take a stand.
You will not find her hard to understand.

My sister, always truthful and outspoken
would never want to see your heart broken.

Picture This

Kelly Young
Rock Springs Middle School, Grade 7

I conceived her vivid likeness
for a pearly dream.
She manifested that birthday
from red-orange facsimiles.

Dependent on the light and mood
her film a delicate veil.
Disguising all the possibilities
of her blooming mind.

I focused on her changing form
intensely delayed by time.
Then the long awaited chance
imprinted on my mind.

Exposed upon the gauzy skin
for every eye to see
The essence of my pride and joy
my husband's epitome.

Circle of Lives

Kerri Clark
Rockvale Elementary School, Grade 5

Do you remember your birth experiences? Mothers enter the hospital, anticipating their new arrival. Families gather and talk about past memories, and those to come. Bright lights shine, monitors flash and beep. The smell of disinfectant is omnipresent, and doctors/nurses give orders. I can recall each experience as if it were yesterday. Each of the three births I experienced was like a new dawn for me.

My first birth experience occurred when I was fifteen. I was present at the birth of my sister. My mom was past the usual childbearing age and I guess her body was playing a joke on her. I was allowed to be in the operating room during the Caesarean delivery of Jamie. I was excited and scared, but boy, was I cool in that green surgical suit! However, I didn't stay cool. Throughout the delivery I had to look up to see the procedure, because my face was buried into my mother's shoulder most of the time. The doctor told me to look up and watch when he reached my sister in my mother's exposed womb, and I did. As he pulled her forth, I thought something was wrong. She was covered in all of this gross stuff. This was not what I imagined birth was like and I was anxious. After her first cry, I was relieved. The nurses took Jamie aside, cleaned her up, and then brought her to us. I was the first to hold Jamie, even before my mother, and from that moment on we were bonded together forever. She was like my own.

My next birth experience occurred eleven years later, the birth of my son Landon. Jamie had always heard of how I was in the delivery room with her, so she wanted to be with me during his delivery. We went to childbirth classes to prepare her. On the day of Landon's delivery, this eleven-year-old child was by my side taking care of me as if she were my own little nurse. My husband and parents marveled at this. When time came, the doctor said we could not deliver in the birthing room, but needed to move to the surgical room. I began to cry, not only from fright, but because their policy would not allow Jamie to go with me. After Landon's birth, they rolled me back and Jamie was the third person to hold him. I shared what I knew was Jamie's disappointment, but when she held him and smiled, I knew everything would be okay.

My final birth experience came four years later. It was the birth of my daughter Kendall, and Jamie was fifteen. This time things would be different. As we prepared in the birthing room, she was playing with Landon, and not planning to stay for the delivery. I pulled her aside and we talked again about the two earlier experiences. I asked her if she wanted to stay for the delivery and she was euphorically happy. Kendall wasn't going to wait for the doctor to arrive, so the nurse delivered her in the birthing room with Jamie and family by my side. Jamie cried when she saw the baby for the first time. She thought something was wrong because she was covered in all of the gross stuff. After hearing her cry out, she realized, as I did, that everything was going to be fine. When the nurse wrapped my new daughter up and asked if I wanted to hold her, I declined and asked Jamie to be the first to hold Kendall, as I had been privileged to do when she was born.

The fifteen-year circle of life that occurred between my sister and me will never be broken. We will forever be close, especially since all three of my birth experiences happened in August with only a seventeen-day difference, and all deliveries by the same doctor. I cannot wait to experience childbirth again one day, this time as a loving witness to my sister's delivery.

Dear Miracle

Kelli Shockey
Rock Springs Middle School, Grade 8

The first day I saw you, I was in total shock. You were the most beautiful, miraculous sight I had ever seen – a tiny peanut of a being with a rapidly beating heart staring back at me from the fuzzy black and white screen. I was witnessing a miracle of God's grace. Ever since that day, my life has been consumed by you. Will you love me as much as I love you? Will you be healthy? What will you be? What will you become?

I have dreams of you – lying in my arms, looking up at me with loyalty and trust and a love so pure that it flows through my body to reside in my soul. The aura of those dreams contains a peace that I have never known and a promise of what is to come. Others say that birth brings about irreversible changes in life, but God has been preparing my heart for you for so long, that I cannot imagine there ever being any other life without you.

I pray that you find love and a peace within yourself, which is the only way to true happiness. I pray that you know God so that you can know the miracles that are in store for you. I pray that you have the confidence to become all the things I never thought I could be. I pray that you know throughout your life that you are loved. I know my prayers will not be in vain.

I can't wait to meet you – to take you on long walks through the woods in the fall, to teach you how to make meatloaf and cornbread the way my mother taught me, to show you where I grew up, to tell you about my dad – your grandfather – whom you will never know, and to whisper "I love you's" into your ear while you dream.

The pain of our earlier loss makes you all the more special, all the more loved. Our other precious hope wasn't in God's plan, but you – you are my miracle – my new hope, my joys, my fears, my heart. God knew that you were the one for us. You are the answer to a prayer, a light in the midst of darkness, a sacred miracle in this scientific, secular world. You are not even here yet, but I feel like I've known you throughout my entire existence. I cannot imagine life without you. Right now, whether you will be a Brayden, a Rheagan, or an Aubrie is inconsequential. Just the fact that you are mine – God's reward for my patience – is all that matters in the world.

My Relatives

Elizabeth Sparkman
David Youree Elementary School, Grade 1

Do your relatives ever come visit? Do you remember them coming to visit when you were a child? Some time ago, I discovered a wonderful, delightful book called "The Day the Relatives Came." I often read this book to my first graders, although in the process, I find myself laughing and crying at the same time. The students, while not totally understanding my reaction to the book, definitely enjoy the story and especially the illustrations. They do not always understand my joy with this book. Let me explain it to you if I can.

I come from a family of eleven children. We are all happy, thriving adults with families of our own now. But there was a time, when we were all living under the same roof at the same time, except for my oldest brother, who was married by the time my youngest brother came along. We were a healthy, God-fearing, respected family in our community.

We had cousins everywhere. My mom's brother had married my dad's sister, and my mom's sister had married my dad's brother. I had double-first cousins that seemed like brothers and sisters. There was a passel of us. It seemed we were everywhere, *those relatives and us!*

There was one set of cousins, however, that lived, what seemed to us as kids a million miles away, in Biloxi, Mississippi. My dad's oldest brother had served in the army in WWII and was stationed near there. While in the service, he met and married a wonderful and sweet woman from that area. Her name was Aunt Marie. Uncle C.M. (as we called him, short for Charlie Mckinley), and Aunt Marie eventually produced nine children of their own. In stair step progressive intervals with my brothers, sisters and myself, *the relatives came!*

Uncle C.M. and Aunt Marie only made it home to Tennessee once a year. They might come in the summer or maybe at Christmas. As I recall it, it was in the heat of the summer, *that the relatives came!*

This was before the time of air-conditioned vehicles, family vans, or mobile-home-size campers, trucks with toppers, or any other vehicle that might have provided a little extra space or comfort for a family of eleven. And it was also before the days of interstates or bypasses. Twisty, curvy, state highways had to be traveled the entire distance. Conceive in your mind's eye, a picture of the old station wagon, with windows rolled down all around, filled to the brim with wiggling, squealing children, hefty teenagers, overworked adults, and left-over bits of balogna sandwiches, and *your vision is complete of how the relatives came!*

When we received word as to when we could expect these cousins of ours, we excitedly looked forward to the day when they would come rumbling down our dusty road for a couple of weeks of unending fun! On the day of their anticipated arrival, we could hardly wait *for the relatives to come!*

Finally, here they came, with arms flailing out the windows. Clothes were stashed in boxes and bags, stored wherever there was an empty space to cram them.

Oh, the celebrating that went on! These cousins of ours, that we had only heard from/or about on leaves of treasured paper throughout the year, were actually here. There seemed to be no end to the hugging and kissing, back-slapping and jostling, all around the yard *when the relatives came!*

My dad and his brother hugged and exchanged a handshake and talked about the trip.

Mom and Aunt Marie immediately embraced and began their lengthy discussions about all us kids, foods that needed to be prepared, their most recent childbirthing experiences, and life in general. And from there, as from my memories I recall, it was all breathtaking and unending *when the relatives came!*

One of my dearest memories is about food. In those days (the late 50's, early 60's), fresh seafood, or any seafood for that matter, was not easy to come by in rural Middle Tennessee. Often Uncle C.M., living near the coast, brought shrimp, or occasionally some other type of seafood. Oh, how I loved that shrimp! But of course, it wasn't an all you can eat meal, just enough to get your taste buds in a rage *when the relatives came!*

My happy, hostess mom, was and still is a wonderful cook! Those nieces and nephews of hers loved her country cooking. Mom made a special recipe called "Chocolate Gravy". Now chocolate gravy is just that. It is a sweet, milk chocolate gravy that is absolutely out of this world when ladled over butter and a homemade buttermilk biscuit. We couldn't believe these cousins of ours never had this at their house. But Aunt Marie said try as she might, she just could not get it right. So, chocolate gravy it was at Aunt Bird's house *when the relatives came!*

At the end of the day, nighttime surely fell, and plans to bed everyone down began. Feather-stuffed pillows and homemade quilts would be dragged from shelves and shared from beds, and pallets were spread all across the house. As the children began to be bedded down and the house became increasingly quiet, the adults gathered to have some uninterrupted visiting. We children drifted off to dream world with the drone of comfortable voices, the outside sounds of crickets and jar flies drifting through opened windows, with contented happy little hearts beating inside our chests! There was such a peacefulness about that whole scene. I guess it seemed our family was complete *when the relatives came!*

The only time as a child I ever saw my Daddy cry were the days the visiting was over and it was time for the relatives to again bag up all their wringer-washer washed, lined-dried clothes, stash them and all the children in the station wagon, and head off to Sparta to visit other members of our extended family, *who were waiting excitedly for the relatives to come!*

Uncle C.M. was the last to crawl into the car. He and Dad shared another hug and handshake. Daddy's nice, white, starched handkerchief, and Uncle C.M.'s wrinkled, somewhat used hanky, were pulled from hip pockets, and tears swiped away *as the relatives prepared to go!*

And we all stood, Mom and Dad and barefoot children, with arms flailing, and watched as that faithful old station wagon pulled from our yard and headed back up that dusty road. No one moved until we could no longer make out individual faces in the windows and only the sound of the departing automobile was left. Then we all turned away to once again find ourselves, and began to look forward to next year *when the relatives would come!*

The Tooth Fairy

Kelly Wester
LaVergne Middle School, Grade 8

I tried my best, I really did, but after having four children my life just got busy. Our first son, Christopher, we never let cry. He was our whole world. He was the first grandchild on either side so he got all the new clothes, new toys, new books and especially all the attention. We were by his side energetically nurturing, guiding, and teaching.

But by the fourth son, we were just doing the best we could. Marky is the baby of the family, and he loves it. As new parents, we tried to do it all, but by the time Marky came along we had relaxed—we just didn't have the time or strength to do it all with two in diapers, Christopher starting school, work, and clubs and activities that we're all involved in. I didn't realize how much we had taken for granted until one day when Marky was in kindergarten. Marky was sitting in front of the TV, and all of the sudden he came running to me terrified.

"Mom, look what happened!" I looked down and in Marky's hand was a small tooth.

"Oh, let me see you smile," I gently prodded. Mark smiled widely and right in the front of his mouth was a small gaping hole. "Your baby tooth came out."

"But I didn't do anything—it just fell out," Marky explained. Knowing Marky, I highly doubted it had just fallen out.

It was then that I realized that even though he had three older brothers, one of whom he shared a room with, Marky didn't know about the Tooth Fairy! How could this be? Even though his older brothers had long since known the truth about the Tooth Fairy, they were still milking it for all the cash they could get.

"Marky, all of your teeth right now are baby teeth," I explained. "Slowly each tooth will fall out and a new tooth will replace it. If you put the baby teeth under your pillow, the Tooth Fairy will come and give you money for your teeth."

"You mean you get money for teeth?" Mark excitedly asked.

"Yes, now put that tooth in an envelope and put it under your pillow. In the morning you can see what the Tooth Fairy leaves you."

As Marky raced away, I was chastising myself that this was one more thing I hadn't explained to him. The boys were growing up too fast, and I couldn't keep up with all those magical times in their lives. I wanted to slow things down and savor each moment.

Marky returned to watching the TV, and I began making dinner. About a half an hour later, Marky again ran up to me. This time he had his hand cupped just below his mouth and there was blood and spit dripping from his mouth. Alarmed, I asked what had happened.

"Now, wiw I gets lots of money?" Marky mumbled through blood and spit.

"What are you talking about?" I asked anxiously. Looking closer at Marky's hand, I saw in it three small teeth. I looked at Mark, and he smiled—all his front teeth were missing.

"Marky, what happened to your teeth?" I asked in horror.

Still grinning Marky replied, "You said the Tooth Fairy gave money for teeth. Am I gonna get a lot for all my teeth?"

I was horrified by the realization of what he had done. Being a child who was already alert to income opportunities, Marky had wiggled those teeth until he could pull them out.

"Yes, you'll get a lot," I said with some chagrin. I cleaned Marky up and then tried to explain that teeth generally come out one or two at a time and usually in six month intervals. It must have been a successful lesson, as he gave up his career in self-dentistry afterward.

Two years passed before Marky's teeth finally grew in. The front two were crowded because they had come out too soon and are now slightly crossed. One of my life lessons is revealed each time I see Marky smile now. Life rushes by so quickly. Am I enjoying each passing moment with all of my sons—or just trying to make it through each day? Slow down, talk to each of them about everything, laugh with them, reflect with them, and savor each and every experience.

Parenthood

Leisa Barrier
Blackman Middle School, Grade 6

Children darting to and fro,
Brother and sister fighting so.
"Mom, come here!" they both shout,
Two different versions as to what the fight's about.
Days are full of tasks and noise,
Parents tripping over toys,
Dishes pile up in the sink,
Seems there's barely time to think.
Dinner's cooked, but the laundry's waiting,
Shirts need folding and socks need mating.
Bath time's over and story time's near,
Quietly listening they seem so dear.
Children tucked safely into bed,
Parents can relax and clear their heads.

Middle School years are busy with academics and sports,
"Mom, did you wash my shorts?
Don't forget my game's tonight.
I invited the team over if that's alright."
The game is over and we're home at last,
Peace and quiet is a thing of the past.
Shouts and laughter, crashing, thumping,
Music blaring and bodies jumping.
Dad groans, "It's 2:00 AM, and I'm still awake,
I don't know how much more I can take."
Mom goes downstairs to quiet the boys,
Thirty minutes later there's just as much noise.
"That's OK, we can sleep the next night,"
They resign themselves to this night's plight.
The next day they receive the news,
Their daughter's friends will be here——just a few.
Screams and giggles, laughing and prancing,
Music blaring and bodies dancing.
Dad and Mom lie awake in bed,
Another sleepless night ahead.
Parents feel joy when their children are cheery,
But these hectic schedules make parents weary.
Homework, projects, sleepovers, and sports are fun,
But often parents say they just need one.

One day to rest at home and do the chores,
Just stay put at home.... no chauffeuring, no sports, no stores.

High School years are busy with academics and sports,
Mom still needs to wash their shorts.
Parents enjoy watching the games,
But somehow its not the same.
Teens are now old enough to drive,
They try to lead independent lives.
The thought of them driving cars fills you with fear,
Parents anxiously awaiting a noise to hear.
It's now silence that keeps the parents awake,
Worrying about possible driving mistakes.
Until their teens arrive home safe and sound,
There is no sleep to be found.

High school graduation is past,
Boy, those years flew by fast!
Once in college their children's presence is sought,
Parents reminisce about their children as tots.
College students often live in a dorm,
So silent evenings are now the norm.
"It's too quiet," the parents complain,
They're looking forward to noise again!
Parents reflect and still want just one day,
One day to once again hear their children laugh and play.
The silent nights that they used to treasure,
No longer seem to bring the same pleasure.

A Wondrous Couple

Diane Kelley
Wilson Elementary School, Grade 3

Dad was such a wonderful Christian gentleman
Who was willing to take a stand.
He loved to sing praises
As he walked through the daisies on his farm.
Rocking on the side porch
With a smile lit up like a torch
He was my friend.
A snowball fight he would challenge
As he came home from work.
Now you're singing in the Heavens
And I will see you again in Glory Land.

Mom is such a wonderful Christian lady
Who reads the Bible and prays
For her daughter, grandchildren, and family.
A smile all aglow with arms reaching out
Frolicking from flowers, garden, and all about
Making sure there was always food on the table
Whether it be peanut butter and crackers or pinto beans
What a friend you are
And I hold you dearly in my heart.

The Untraditional Family

Tracy Linnell
Stewartsboro Elementary School, Grade 5

The nine-year-old girl jumped from her mom's car. She immediately began to play with the baby as her mom discussed details with the baby's beautiful, young mother. The girl's mom appeared nervous about leaving her with the woman who had stolen her husband and ripped her family apart, yet she wanted her child know her dad. This woman now had visiting rights to her only child. The young mother with the perfect hair and makeup like a star radiated confidence and coolness to the naïve young girl. The girl excited about the new baby and finally spending time with her dad exchanged "byes" with her mom. The weekend was going to be an extraordinary glimpse at the "all-American family" thought the young girl. Friday night went quickly in the small trailer. The trailer on the outskirts of town with no TV or phone didn't bother the young girl hoping to experience "family." The night did not produce the dad she had been missing at home. Saturday dragged on as the newness of the baby began to evolve into a chore. The once beautiful step-mom appeared this morning as an unsure, scared teen who confided in the child that the dad didn't come home and the milk was running low. The Saturday sun rose and set with no dad gracing the door. Sunday opened for the young girl with a gentle but urgent shake from the step-mom. The delicate threesome dressed and began a journey to the closest store for milk. As they walked nervously by the busy highway a car screeched to a halt. A familiar head emerged from the window. It was dad, but not the "all-American" dad for whom she had been waiting, just an unkempt, hung over, smelly man calling her baby. The step-mom screamed as the smelly man yelled back, while the young girl and baby watched. Finally, the threesome joined the man in the car and they continued to the store. However, they did not turn around as one would think. The man put the car in reverse and eased into the other lane. They continued in reverse until they reached the store. The girl holding the baby in the back had numerous thoughts and emotions searing through her mind and body. The screaming lingered on until the threesome was dropped at the front door of the trailer. The car sped away as did the "all-American family" the young girl had dreamt of so many times.

Waiting
Patsy L. Slusher
Eagleville School, Grade 5

The police cars with lights and sirens blaring, motorcycles roaring, and large buses with soldiers waving, passed our location. As I stood by the side of the road with my sister to welcome home Murfreesboro's National Guard soldiers returning from Iraq, I could not help but recall another homecoming many years ago.

My junior year in college had been difficult. My family was scattered. My mother had been transferred to Florida, Joyce lived in Philadelphia, Susanne in Washington, D. C., Jo in Tampa, and Gary was serving in Vietnam. I felt abandoned because I was the only one of my immediate family left in Middle Tennessee.

As the year progressed, visions of war protests on college campuses were broadcast daily - buildings burning, windows breaking, pushing, shoving, shouting. Would this occur on my campus? We would awake every morning to peak out the window to see if anything had happened the night before. Would I be forced to watch my fellow students jeer my brother? Only time would tell.

The year was creeping to an end. How much longer would it be before he returned? Finally I received a phone call from my mother; however, it was not the news I wanted.
She would drive up tomorrow because Papa, my grandfather, was in the hospital with spinal meningitis. Disappointment and dread filled me.

Several nerve-racking days passed as Papa gradually recovered. I knew he would survive. A spark of happiness flickered inside. "At least one good thing occurred!" I thought. As I lay on my bed wasting time after class, Mother paid me a surprise visit. "There's someone downstairs who wants to see you?" she whispered.

Immediately I knew! I bounded down three flights, running to the lobby of my dorm. There he was. No "Welcome Home" signs. No parades. No marching bands. No sirens blaring. No American flags waving in the air.

He was home.
He was safe.
He was my brother!

TYLER

June Culp
Blackman Middle School, Grade 8

T is for the thesaurus of towering ideas stored in your mind.
Y is for the youthful yearning to learn all that you can.
L is for the lucid light you shine in my life.
E is for the physical exercise, which I have finally convinced you is expedient.
R is for the reassuring relationship you have with your
L ord and Savior.

TYLER, a gift from God and my son – I love you!

Having My Say

Vzea Foster
Buchanan Elementary School, Grade 6

I sometimes ponder when I look at you and know that time has a way of catching us all. For me, this is a startling thought because I can't imagine life to be any different; perhaps we will fall.

I often reflect on situations in my life and think how would mama handle this? But it's amazing to know human emotions will show, and we all make mistakes you do know.

It surprises me how much you love your grandchildren seeing no wrong that they do. When we endured punishments that was always thorough as you do what you normally do. When I tell you of horrors about their wrongdoings you would only say, "Oh, how cute!" I say to myself, "Is this the woman I knew?"

I know you miss daddy a lot even though things got really tough. You endured because you felt you should and spent more than fifty years of your life.

Now you have a relationship with your "Father," one you seem to hold on high. It seems to get you through the day and comfort you through the night.

I wonder how you did it when you raised all of us... some good times some bad, but knowing you gave it your best. I only hope to be able to hold my head up high the way that you do when speaking of life's treasures; to be able to follow in your footsteps would give me much pleasure.

My Four Sons (The Now)

Joyce Hugle
Wilson Elementary School, Grade 3

Dear Sons,

Have I told you how I feel about you? Probably not always in words but hopefully in my actions. Do we have a close bond as parent and child? I think so; do you? Can we discuss personal things as well as every day affairs? Sometimes yes and sometimes no. Are we always in agreement with everything we talk about? Sometimes yes, but often times, no.

Now you are adults ages 38, 35, 34, and 28 with your own futures and destinies at hand.

First born son: Being 38 and the oldest you are a true and good example for your brothers to follow. You followed the path most parents dream for their child. You completed high school and college, obtained a job, and chose to wed your soul-mate. Now rearing a child, seemingly you have been placed in your purpose.

Second born son: Age 35, married with five children. You are a "can-do-it-all" son. You are the one we all call on when we need something fixed or done. You attended college for a while, then decided to seek employment. You have continued to search for that right job. Hopefully you are on the right path now.

Third born son: Age 34 and married with three children. You are a "fatherly figure" and the worker of the sons. You attended college for some time and worked in various job settings. You are able to adjust to mostly any situation. Prayerfully, you're ready for the future, now.

Fourth born son: Age 28 and single and a college graduate. You are now working on a job until you land the job of your dreams. You are a "good-hearted" person and level-headed too. You are always her for me and for others. Faithfully, your dreams will be fulfilled.

Now, with this said, although we have faced a few obstacles and successes, I'm proud to be to each of you – your Mother.

Mama/Joyce

Dear Grama

Carrie E. Perkins
Riverdale High School, Grades 9-12, Art

Dear Grama,

      I've not been by your spot of rest in many years but there is not a day, and I do mean day, that your words don't ring out through my mind, as well as your children and grandchildren's mouths. When our family is in flux, despair or celebration, we all look to your input and wisdom. You gave me so many tangible and intangible gifts; Grama, your quiet hand in church, your sayings that ring so true and your knowledge and skill around a sewing table that echoes and rebounds when my mother and I create over her canvas table. The latest gift I received from you was my own letter back, missing a page! What a wonderful mystery; as though you kept a part of it for yourself when you left us fifteen years ago, a letter that I remember writing as a homesick eight-year-old wishing for love and acceptance in a new place. You kept this letter, you kept a piece of my heart that you had to know would return to me when I most needed it. My mother, the re-affirmation of what a mother is, returned my letter you left for me because she is such a wonderful reflection of you. Our connections as women in this family seem so tangible, so rock-solid and grounded around you.

      Thank you, for being with me everyday, through my thoughts and choices.

Love ya,
Carrie

Flea

D'ann Cooper
Smyrna Elementary School, Grade 5

Flea is a nickname given to a boy
who followed along bringing lots of joy.

This little boy was sure to hide
always by Coach Danny's side.

Coach Danny is the one
who gave this nickname to my son.

Who'd ever thought
this name would have stuck with a tot?

Spencer Lee or Spencer Flea?
Guess which one Spencer would be proud for it to be?

I'm a Sixth Grader

Jennifer Dawson
Christiana Middle School, Grade 6

Dear Mom and Dad,

I am going into sixth grade this year, no longer a child like I was in fifth, but not quite as grown up as the seventh graders I've met in our neighborhood. I'm going to need some things this year that may seem strange and foreign to you, but perfectly sensible to me.

First, after examining the latest issue of any teen magazine, I will let you know what clothes we should be shopping for as well as the haircut I would like to have this year – or at least for the next couple of months. Clothing and hairstyles come in and out of style rather quickly, so please do not be alarmed if I change my mind by Christmas. I will also need to be supplied with lots of cool gadgets and organizers to help me become an organized teen. I love highlighters, colored pens, decorative folders and any other items that will help me to be creative, yet organized, this year (but don't count on it actually happening).

I would also ask that you show me patience as I begin this new journey into middle school and eventually to high school. My teachers tell me I have to be responsible for my own things and actions. but I can still use some help from you until I fully step out on my own with this. I know I've ALWAYS had A's but I'm just trying to adjust to five teachers with different homework assignments and expectations. I need to be compared to the best I can do, not the best others can do. I know I'm not the person you have known for years, but I will soon grow into someone you will like equally as well.

As far as my personal life goes, please remember that talking endlessly (about nothing really important to adults) on the phone nightly is crucial to my development. Life in middle school is truly about "who is doing what" and "what we should wear tomorrow" and it MUST be discussed. I need guidance to be able to understand how to draw the line between being nice to others so I do not hurt their feelings and when to stick up for what I believe in. I would like you to drop me off at the school dance coming up, but please do not volunteer to chaperone. I'd hate for you to see that I can dance in ways other than what I learned at "Helen's School of Dance." Please do not be alarmed if I come home crying or upset some days. It really is a tragedy when someone is mad at you…but it will be okay as tomorrow we will all make up. I only need to realize that it is understandable to be angry, and I have a right to be. However, I have no right to be cruel to others because of my anger. I also need help to understand that I should not change friends just because they change. It is hard to put who a person is in front of his actions sometimes and I'm just learning this. On the relationship side of things, you may have never heard the term "going out." It means I really like someone enough to call him or her a boyfriend or girlfriend. We may never actually go anywhere, but we can pretend.

I'd like to be a part of a club or team sport, but I need you to help me prioritize my schedule. I never realized how demanding a young adult's schedule can be. Please remember I need lots of praise at this time in my life, although I can't really pinpoint the cause, some days just seem harder than others. We are learning about hormones in health class. I think this might be the key to this "up days, down days thing." I will also be glad to have the encouragement to be a leader when I am in the midst of uncertainty. I don't need to stumble over other's mistakes but make and learn from my own. I hope I can learn from you and from living this year that it is not what I profess, but what I practice, that will define my integrity.

There is one last thing to remember this year. I'm going to bring you new and exciting moments each day. I will be growing from someone on the brink of puberty to being a full-blown teen by the end of the year. So please do not be surprised by anything I might do this year...just remember, I'm a sixth grader.

Love,
Your Child

Father's Day

Jeff Duke
Homer Pittard Campus School, Grade 6

Father's Day is rapidly approaching. As I ponder on what to do for this annual event, I realize I have to check by family's busy schedule and try to pencil in a visit to my father as part of my responsibility as a loyal son. I'm sure that the person or people who made Father's Day an annual event did not intend for this day of observance to be something else to do as part of our already busy lives. This is a day that we should celebrate our fathers. Not until I became a father myself did I realize that fathers everywhere have earned a day to be honored and revered. We deserve it.

As I was growing up, my father was a man of few words. He communicated very effectively without saying anything. You learned to tell what he was thinking by the way he stood, certain facial expressions, and then there was "the stare." "The stare" brought on its victims an array of feelings. Fear, anxiety, respect, and the contemplation of potential pain were just a few of the emotions you would feel when "the stare" was used by my dad. You knew he meant business and you'd better react accordingly.

From my perspective as a child, my dad often seemed to be angry and in a bad mood, and I wondered why this was the case. My brother, sisters, and I would ask ourselves a variety of questions when my dad arrived home. Is he in a good mood? Did I do anything I was not supposed to do? Did I do everything I was supposed to do? These are some of the questions that would pop to our minds. We didn't want to be around if any of these questions could be answered with a negative response by anyone of us.

Even though my dad seemed to be angry and in a bad mood a great deal, I never doubted his love for us. We knew we could always count on him for help. If truth be known, he very rarely spanked us. "The stare" was punishment enough.

As a parent myself I finally made a connection with what my dad went through as a father. He worked two jobs for most of his life to provide for us. Dad wanted to make sure that we knew the difference between right and wrong. He also wanted to instill in us that everyone deserves respect; especially those people who guide and lead us down the right path of life. Most of all, Dad wanted us to be obedient to God and realize the importance of being good Christian people. This is a great deal to think about, and I understand the stress he went through as a father.

When I first heard my mother say a few years ago, "You act just like your father," I was horrified. When I first recognized for myself that I acted just like my father, I was speechless. As I have grown older and obviously wiser I have come to the realization that being like my father is not such a bad thing after all. In fact, in the last few years he has become one of the wisest persons I have ever known. It's funny how your perspectives change as you mature.

Over the years I have seen my dad amazingly mellow. He seems happier since my brother, sisters, and I moved out on our own. (I wonder why that is?) Now that he has grandchildren, he is a totally different person. He spoils them rotten, and they can do no wrong. Life appears to have new meaning for my father.

After seventeen years of fatherhood, I have arrived at the point where I'm looking forward to my children moving out and living on their own. I am also looking forward to grandchildren I can spoil and send home when they get on my nerves. Most of all, I'm looking forward to the moment that my children realize I am one of the wisest people they have ever known. In fact, I think fathers need more than one day a year to be recognized. Lets face it. Mothers only have one day. Fathers only have one day. Children have 363 days. Something is wrong with this picture. So to fathers everywhere everyday, "HAPPY FATHER'S DAY!!!"

The Two-Way Mirror

Ann Hughes
Siegel High School, Grades 11 and 12

I sometimes feel as if I'm a two-way mirror between my dear parents and my sweet son. I'm a reflection of them, and he's a reflection of us. As parents of two girls, my parents have received this grandson with joy and, at times, consternation. "The boy," as he is often referred to by my father, has been blessed with extra servings of forthrightness, mischievousness, and acuteness.

As the daughter of these two individuals, I have great insight as to what my mother and father consider acceptable and heathenish behavior. I am well aware of where their golden buttons are and just how far to push them. Also, as a *grown woman* who lives under her *own roof* and pays her *own bills*, I sometimes, oh who am I kidding, I always take wicked delight in seeing Mama and Daddy squirm when their chains get rattled now and then.

As the folks often remind me, I seem to be "paying for my raising." This has proven to be true on a staggering number of occasions. "Yes, Daddy, it's true. 'The boy' did fight at the family reunion, and yes, he did claim he intended to 'bring blood' with that stick." However, if I'm paying for my raising, the grandparents haven't gotten off scot-free either. "Oh, Mama, calm down! He's four, and you don't even know those people. By tomorrow they will have forgotten the little boy who announced that you broke wind in aisle 7." Oh yes, in my eyes, Granny and Joe Daddy are settling their own accounts for *how* they raised me, and sometimes when "the boy" is stretching for those buttons and grasping at chains, smugly I think, "Go, boy, go!"

At such deliciously satisfying times when the chains have been stretched taut by chubby little hands against my parents' collars and tinges of pink embarrassment or shades of purple aggravation creep onto the faces just above those collars, I very quietly fade into the silvery nothingness of that two-way mirror to watch the future reflect and do battle with the past.

Gifts From a Mother

Celinda Miller
Siegel Middle School, Grade 6

Dear Alex,

As I sit down today I find myself thinking of gifts. Our world is full of items that can be bought with money and given as gifts. Certainly, most people take pleasure in giving and receiving gifts. However, the gifts I want to give you cannot be bought with money. They cannot be ordered from a store or from the internet. The gifts I want to give to you come from my heart. These gifts will last longer than the latest toy or electronic game you will ever receive in your life.

The first gift I give to you is the gift of love. Certainly, love is the reason you are here today. You come from two very loving parents who will always love you, no matter what may occur in your life. The gift of family and friends is precious. You have been so blessed in your life to have others who love you; grandparents, aunts, uncles, cousins, and a multitude of friends. I wish for you to be filled with love-not only for others, but also for yourself. Always remember that it is important to love yourself. Paired with the gift of love is the gift of compassion. Compassion means caring about others. It means to think of other people and to not think only of yourself. You will meet many people in your lifetime who may be less fortunate than you, whether, perhaps, in money, a home, or possessions. Be willing to give love to others even if they may seem unlovable to you. Having love for yourself and others will make you a better person.

The second gift I give to you is the gift of responsibility. Being responsible means taking care of things on your own. You may have the responsibility of taking care of a pet, taking care of your room, or taking care of work at school or at home. Develop good self-discipline, a facet of being responsible. These gifts, after all, are all a parent can truly give any child. You are only on loan to us for a short time. There will be times your father and I will not be able to take care of things for you as we have done while you were small. Also, remember that the world and other people do not owe you anything. You will need to work for the things you want. You will need to develop responsibility for self-control. This includes being responsible for your behavior and the things you say whether it is at home or away from your parents. Be responsible with money. Don't try to have things or buy things that you cannot afford. Don't spend your money just because you have it. Always have some saved for emergencies or just for fun times. Be as giving with your money as you are with your talents. Think of ways you can help others quietly with your money. A true giver doesn't always have his name in writing. Sometimes, the silent givers are the most generous.

The third gift I give to you is the gift of education. Don't ever take your education for granted. Right now, you are learning something new every day even though you haven't started school yet. Life is an education in itself. Take advantage of any learning opportunities you are given. Your father and I have seen to it that you have had many advantages to see different places and things already, and we will continue to do so in the future. Continue to develop your love of reading. There are whole worlds waiting out there for you between the covers of books. Learn to read, and you can do anything you want in life. There are opportunities for learning in the world around you. One day you may wish to go to college to further your education. Work hard to achieve your dreams and believe anything is possible even if it seems there is little to no money for college. Your father and I will be here to help you as much as we can but learn to rely on yourself for the money. Work hard in school so that you may take opportunities for scholarships. Going to college will give you the opportunity to make choices about your life and what you wish to become.

The fourth gift I give you is the gift of respect. In our world today it may seem that respect is not important. However, it is one of the most important qualities you can have. Have respect for others whether they are adults or other persons your own age. More importantly, have respect for yourself. If you do not respect yourself, how can you expect others to respect you? Having respect means thinking of others and choosing your actions and words carefully before acting upon them. Respect includes addressing others as "sir" and "ma'am" and also listening to people when they are advising you. You will be faced many times in your life where being respectful may not be the "in" thing to do. Remember to be respectful anyway and you will come out the winner in the end.

Another gift I give to you is the gift of my time. Our time together is precious. I give us time to laugh, cry, snuggle up with a good book, and a time to listen. Don't take the gift of time for granted. Make every day count and live for today. Time is something God gives us.

My final gift to you is the gift of being yourself. Don't be afraid to stand up for what you believe in. You will meet people in your lifetime who will not agree with your feelings and who will try to get you to change to their way of thinking. Stand firm in your beliefs even if you are the only one standing. Be considerate of others but be faithful to yourself.

My wish is that you will accept these gifts from me. You may never become wealthy or win an award for these gifts. However, I hope these gifts will help you have a wonderful and blessed life and that one day you can say, "My life has been the best because of these gifts I received from a loving mother."

Love,
Mommy

Dad

Marcella O. B. Watts
Blackman Elementary School, Grade 3

In his younger days, dad stood six feet two and a half inches tall, but when I was a smallish ten years old, he seemed much taller. He had a very commanding presence. Unexpectedly I witnessed him make a grown man cry like a newborn that lacks milk. He was highly respected in his community and in church. As long as I could remember I'd been afraid of Dad. I cannot explain why or how it ever began. I do recall believing if he could make a grown man cry, or considered a tree branch a switch, that he was serious business. I also reflected on the times I heard him remark, "Are you bleeding? If you're not bleeding then don't cry." "A 'C' is the same as an 'F'." I also hear echoing in my ear. My fear was not diminished by the presence of a thick bumpy evergreen belt that hung on a special hook. Although I never felt it, I knew I had cause to fear. I quaked to see his extremely stern face and grimacing eyebrows as he pointed to my room. Those eyes are powerful and unforgettable. They compelled me once to take undeserved blame, well, I actually confessed to over-stuffing the toilett when I didn't even do it.

Dad worked very hard. He would leave before daybreak and would quit working long after the moon chased the sun away. He was an excellent provider of life's necessities. However, if a complaint was heard about the need or lack of something, the typical response from Dad was: "My fixing cars is what feeds and clothes you." No, Dad was not a mechanic. He was an engineer for Avco, later Textron. To say he was a workaholic is a grave understatement. Whenever he moved from one level to the next at Avco, it took two men to fill his spot. Once it took THREE men to fill the ONE position he left. When the workday was done at Avco he came home, changed from suit and tie to overalls and left to fix cars, his work-based form of relaxation. I can keenly remember the thick black dirt ever present under his nails. I can still smell the embedded motor oil stained work clothes he wore.

One day I packed the dishwasher and turned it on to clean. I still had a few things to accomplish in the kitchen before my chore was complete, so I began to wipe off the tables and put things away. After a moment or two I noticed that soapsuds were all over the floor. They were flowing from the dishwasher! Who knew that dish soap wouldn't work the same? While the suds were running across the floor from the machine I did what any fear filled panicking child would do: I ran away!

I went to my room, packed a suitcase and promptly wrote a four-part note to my parents. After placing it around my room like a scavenger hunt, I quietly padded down the hall and out the garage door. Once outside, I didn't know where to go. Thoughts of my stupidity were the only ones I had. I knew I had to leave, but where would I go? Anxiously, and with much desperation, I

144

began to run. I kept running until I reached an abandoned car in the woods behind our home. I jumped in and cried myself to sleep. It was a hopeless slumber.

As I uneasily slept, I was awakened by sounds of tapping on glass. As I opened my eyes and lifted my tear stained face I looked into those eyes! I could barely look. I was frozen with fear. I sat up as my father opened the door and climbed into the back seat. He looked at me. I don't remember all he said or even what I said. All I remember are those eyes peering at me. A previously unrecognized compassion and love were reflected there and I will always remember the man who made men cry asked me to come home. Those newfound eyes forgave me and he told me that home would not be the same without me.

A Letter to My Unborn Child

April Foster
Smyrna Middle School, Grade 7

June 15, 2004

Dear Future Son,

As I sit here at a teacher in-service, I can't keep my mind off of you - and it doesn't help that one of your tiny limbs keeps poking my right side. I have dreamed of you since I was a child, holding my first doll, and in less than five weeks I will meet you for the very first time. Gently, I will stroke your face, kiss you, and whisper, "I love you." Each day, I venture into your room to rearrange your tiny clothes or picture you asleep in your crib. Your daddy and I can't wait for the big day! You're the ultimate expression of our love, a piece of him and a piece of me. How I look forward to seeing the beautiful being God has placed within me!

With eternal love,
Your mommy

A Special Mom

Pam Morgan
Blackman Elementary School, Grade 2

I'm a special mother. One might say, "All mothers are special!" Some say that I was chosen to have a "special" child. Well, sometimes I wonder how and why I was chosen. Maybe one day I will know, but for now, I will continue to take one day at a time, try and smile each day, and watch as my daughter brings joy to others.

On November 10, 1981, I was so excited! I was 28 years old and had a baby girl. She was my second child. My son was four. When the nurse brought her into me, I looked at her and I knew something was terribly wrong. While I had a normal delivery, a mother's instinct told me something was not right. Little did I know on that cold morning in November my life would change forever.

Feelings of anger, guilt, and jealously began to consume me. The doctors could not give me any answers. Was it something I had done? What did I do to deserve this? No one could give me any answers. Long trips to hospitals and doctors drained me emotionally and physically. My friends became distant, and my four year old son was so confused. He was not getting the attention from me that he deserved. He had lots of questions that I could not answer.

On July 8, 1982, at 7:15 P.M. I was reading a story to my son. My daughter slept beside me. The phone rang with the news I had been waiting so long to hear. It was not good news. I started crying even before I heard the news. I could tell by the tone of the doctor's voice that my fears were true. The reason my daughter had developmental delays and trouble seeing were due to an abnormality in her brain. I did not hear any of the detailed explanation after that. I just remember asking the doctor, "What can we do for her?" and he immediately said in a soft, kind voice, "Give her lots of love." He could not even tell me that she would be able to see, talk, walk, or learn.

The learning part of his last words were especially hard because I was a teacher. I went into a deep depression. I was trying to teach school, trying to take care of my son who was so confused about his sister, and working desperately to keep my family together. I felt so alone; friends did not know what to say to me. My family was supportive, but they were unsure of how to handle the situation. I was not ready to accept the fact that my child was different, and even though I knew she was, I could not face the fact that her life would be so difficult, and so would mine. All of the dreams of gymnastics, college, and a wedding were shattered. Nightmares of wheelchairs, doctors, hospitals, and my daughter living in a sightless world were all I could imagine.

After several months of feeling bitterness and guilt, I received a phone call. The call came from a special school where we lived. I remember her comforting words so clearly.

"We're here for you. We know what you are going through. Please come and look at our school. We've heard about your daughter, and we want to help." That was the day my life began. I went to see the school, and I saw children with all kinds of disabilities. I saw caring teachers , and I saw parents who were in the same situation I was in. Oh yes, I saw happiness and love not only in the students'eyes but also on the faces of the teachers and the parents. At that point I realized that our lives would be fine; we would survive. Life for all of us would be difficult, but we could do it! It would be up to me to lead us through the storm.

Years have passed. Twenty-two years to be exact. Our lives have not been easy. But we have survived. My precious baby daughter is now a beautiful young lady. She has beautiful blond hair, and a smile that can brighten anyone's bad day.

While her vision is limited, she did not have to learn Braille. She reads well, uses a calculator for math, and does various jobs at her sheltered workshop. While her balance is unsteady, she finally started walking at age seven (on Thanksgiving Day!) Kelly is a very happy person. I asked her if she had one wish, what would it be. She replied, "I would love to ride a bike!" What a small wish for a girl with so many problems!

No one could have ever prepared me for this mysterious chapter of my life. I have been truly blessed with two beautiful children. At age 50, I am so thankful for all my blessings. I am now in a support group of parents who have children with special needs.

I have found over the years that help is right around the corner. It might be a friend, a teacher, a family member, or a stranger. Just knowing that others care makes everything OK. When you are handed a bad situation, make the best of it. You won't be able to change it, just weather through it. Smile a lot, cry a little, and be thankful for your blessings every day. Maybe I am special after all!

Dreams Really Do Come True

Mary Catherine Conrad
Smyrna Primary School, Kindergarten

We were at a carnival in the dog days of summer. You must have been about one year old. The whole family was there, sweaty and stinky and loving it! We had the whole place to ourselves. No lines to wait in for food, rides, or the restroom. This was the perfect family outing, or so it seemed at the time.

I remember that Daddy was pushing you in the canopied, umbrella stroller while we watched in suspense as the oldest boys rode a roller coaster that was meant to shake, rattle, and roll ten years off one's life in sixty seconds. We were waving and hollering up at them each time they jerked past us at 50 mph. Memaw and Pawpaw were peering through the camera lens watching the little ones squeal with delight during a train ride that crept around a twenty-foot oval track with two tiny dips. Yet, you could tell it was the most invigorating experience of their young lives so far. The other adults were salivating over a fresh, steaming funnel cake smothered in powdered sugar!

Daddy and I continued meandering through the midway. All the while he was pushing you with one hand and holding my hand with the other. We enthusiastically played all the ridiculously expensive games that are always "fixed" to rarely award a cheap prize, and we moaned over a luscious, sticky caramel apple. We came to a music arena so we took the opportunity to rest a moment in the shade and to let you run around.

I was bending over to let you out when I stopped in my tracks and had to catch my breath at what I saw. I saw your face, my daughter, for the very first time. Your golden curls framed your angelic face. Your big, heavenly blue eyes were beaming up at me with anticipation at the prospect of getting to run and play. Your chubby cheeks were pushed up in the widest, toothless grin. You were clapping your hands in excitement and even squeaking with glee! The sunrays peaking all around you made you appear as a true angel from heaven. I stood there crying at your immense beauty, knowing you were mine, a true gift from God, and Jason.

Then your glorious image began to fade from my vision. It was then that I woke up from this dream of all dreams, kissed your Daddy, and told him that I met our little girl. I immediately branded that picture of you in my memory forever. Although, I knew I would see your face again someday and hold you in my arms and heart forever.

One week later I discovered I was pregnant with you. I didn't need the ultrasound to tell me you were a girl, but it was a reassuring affirmation of the truth in my heart that I had not shared with anyone. I wanted, needed, this dream to come true.

I am so blessed to have met you in my dreams, Sarah Grace. Thank you for giving me that eternal gift of a glimpse in the future. Today you are nine weeks old and more beautiful than I dreamed that night. I will never again doubt that dreams really do come true.

In Memory

Marcella O.B. Watts
Blackman Elementary School, Grade 3

"Zacheus was a wee little man and a wee little man was he..."
Pushing, Running, Go, Go, Go
Short burst of air escape my lungs
Ankles hurt, feet burn, sweat pours down my face
Swollen fingers, body aches, hands that aren't mine
Why do I put myself through this pain?
Nannie, Mary, Marcellus.

White sneakers two sizes too big
Swish; swish back and forth beating the pavement with force
Hair's wet, teeth clinch, tears fill my eyes
1 mile, 2 miles, 3 miles, 4, only 11 more miles to go!
Up hill, down hill, turn this corner
Why? Oh, why do I do this to myself?
Nannie, Mary, Marcellus.

Writing, Reading, Rewriting more
Sending e-mails, letters, and calling all to make sure
Meeting faces, going new places, weekly receiving postcard directions.
Putting myself on the line by telling others about my cause
Wanting them to care, too about something I need to do.
Why do I trust that I'll reach this goal?
Nannie, Mary, Marcellus.

4:30 A.M. on Saturday morning darkness all around.
The only sound I hear is the C-Pap machine of my husband
Roll over, get up, pop pills, drink water, read Bible,
Pray, pack, wet hair, get dressed, brush teeth, and oh yeah,
Got to drink those Emerald Greens!
Why am I up this early?
Nannie, Mary, Marcellus.

5:50 A.M. put the suitcase in the car and hang the dress on the side
Now I must be ready to go.
Drive to Nashville, Brentwood, White House, wherever.
Read the directions while checking the clock.
Gasoline is spent with each passing mile
Why do I put these miles on my car?
Nannie, Mary, Marcellus.

6:50 A.M. I'm here and raring to go!
Where's the path? Who's leading? Will I get lost?
Okay let's go! Walk, Run, Walk, Run
Crowds pass me by. Walk, Run, Walk, Run
Pass others as I go. Walk, Run, Walk, Run
Tell me again why I do this.
Nannie, Mary, Marcellus.

Be careful what you wish for.
Be careful what you ask;
I've got it, and now I must push harder than ever!
I sweat. I bleed. I run through blisters and tears.
I stretch and bend my will as I please.
Why do I push myself towards breaking?
It's for Nannie, Mary, and Marcellus.

Daddy's Girl

Malinda Elledge
Smyrna Middle School, Grade 7

     I have many friends who were, like me, Daddy's girl. They tell stories about football games, trips to the auto mechanic, and secret fast food outings. My dad rarely took me to such mundane places. My dad took me to the butcher. A few blocks from our house there was a diminutive, white plaster storefront with the word Halal painted in black letters above the doorway. My dad and I would drive up to the store in our VW van. As soon as we got out, we could smell the heavy, raw scent of meat housed in an unair-conditioned building. If we arrived when supplies had run low, we could hear the sounds of a goat bleating desperately as it was bled in the alley. We entered through the homemade screen door with rapturous anticipation. A slightly heavy, middle-aged Indian man would greet us with enthusiasm and ask, "What can I get for you today, Reverend Upton?" My dad would survey the skinned carcasses suspended over the blood drenched, concrete floor. He would point to a fat flank or a tender muscle and say, "Five kilograms of that, please." One of the white-coated assistants would immediately take a machete and begin hacking away at whatever slab my father had pointed to. Pieces of fat and bone would fly as meat was thrown onto the unwashed scales until my father's orders were met. After his cuts were wrapped in old newspapers, my father could lean down to me and ask, "What would you like, sweetheart?" I had two standard replies, "Silverside" and "Hamburger." Silverside was my favorite for taste – delicious tender beef that my father would grill over hot charcoal in a converted oil drum. Hamburger was for fun. If I asked for that, Dad would choose some more cuts which would be thrown into the heavy, metal meat grinder at home and emerge in strings of red and white minced meat. It may have been my imagination, but the butcher always seemed to give a little bit extra on my cuts and wrap them more gently. Our purchases complete, we would bid farewell to the smiling butcher and climb back into the van. On the bumpy ride home we would discuss with excitement how we would tell Mom about what great deals we got. Later, there would be trimming, tenderizing, marinating, and grilling. Of course, Daddy's girl helped with that too.

Heaven Sent

Sheila "Diane" Giles
Smyrna Primary School, Grade 3

Grandma,

Remember how you would hold me tight with all your might – as if you couldn't hug hard enough – or the many times you took time out of your busy day to take me aside with gentle hands to show me the skills of that day—such as milking old Bessy the cow, or how about the many times I stood under the huge, old elm tree watching you with awe—as you carried chopped wood in your hand-sewn (MULTI-purpose) apron and carefully built a fire under the huge black kettle. There, with unique precision, you would manage to pour just the right amount of lye soap into the boiling water for the washing of Grandpa's work clothes that he'd worn out in the fields the day before.

Grandma,

Just this past weekend, a little one stood by my side, as I once did with you. We were just standing there inside the basement door, peering outside beyond the protection of the opened basement door as we gazed upon the rain as it gently fell to the ground. Within minutes, watching her eager eyes, I caught myself saying those words, "Go ahead. You can. It's okay. I'm right here." There I stood watching our precious, little "Grand"baby playing in the rain, and in some small way I sensed you did too.

I love you Grandma. Sent to Heaven above from your granddaughter and great-great-"Grand"daughter Paradyse.

An Unanswered Cry

Rosanna Johnson
Thurman Francis Arts Academy, Grade 5

There comes a time in one's life when we feel we must reflect in order to connect with missing pieces of the puzzle in our lives. That painful nudge that just won't go away and causes us to weep with sadness as it creeps in and out of our thoughts day after day. The thought that something is missing and we can't quite figure out what dreadful, dark shadow lurks around the corner.

And then it comes to us waiting patiently…. I always knew that you disliked me, but I didn't understand why. I was only a child and you were the adult. Despite your unkind words, and deliberate acts to shame me, I still tried to win your love. Why did you decide to adopt me? Why did you pretend as if, you, weren't in pain?

All I ever wanted was your affection, for you to reach out to me. All I ever wanted was to feel the prominence of my father's love. Often times in my life I remember watching my friends and their fathers' relationships. How their fathers taught them those many lessons in life to help little girls grow into women, that I will never come to know.

There were so many times when I tried to cry out to you and ask for you to answer my questions that went unanswered. Now that you are no longer here, I'm left to figure out these unanswered questions alone. Maybe it is a part of God's plan for me to never know the true answers. And, though I may never find what I'm essentially looking for to help me along my journey, I do know that I have always loved you; there's never been any doubt, for you are my father.

A Letter
Deborah Sitnikoff
Rockvale Elementary School/McFadden School of Excellence, Band

Remember when you took me to the movies and smuggled that huge bag of cheese puffs under your coat? I was so embarrassed and thought we'd get into so much trouble. I don't know how they never noticed. Maybe the teenage ushers were afraid to confront such a big over-sized scruffy looking man. Or, maybe they were afraid to come close to you, because you were so weird and smelled so bad. Why were you afraid to use soap anyway? I have never understood that. My mom says that a long time ago you owned your own barbershop and were one of the best barbers in town. How did you loose it? I have seen a couple of your pictures then. You were so handsome. I remember you eating those cheese puffs with your nervous hands getting orange dust all over your coat and the theater chair and how you kept dropping the puffs on the floor. You kept asking me if I wanted some, but your hands were so dirty. I was afraid to get your germs. Was it because the medication affected the nerves in your hands?

Did you know that after all these years I have your silver dollar coin collection? When Grumpie died Aunt Pam, my mom, (who were named trustees of my grandpa's estate), and I went through his old file cabinet down in the basement. Behind the collection of pocketknives and 2-dollar bills they found your coins! I think Pam wanted to take that home with her too, but I stood up for my mom and myself and said, "I want to take my Dad's collection home now." I kept repeating the same thing over about three times. "It's all I have from my dad to give my boys someday." Then Pam didn't have much to say. Down in the plastic bag was the jar that you would put your tips in, and it was still full. My mom said when you were in the hospital before the divorce, she was forced to sell a lot of things for food and rent. Instead of my mom selling the collection for food, Grumpie offered to loan her $50. She was to pay him back and he would return the collection. She paid him back a long time ago, but he never wanted to give it back to her when he was living.

People say that little girls grow up and marry men just like their fathers. I have always wondered how that could be true for the girls who were never really around their dads much. Is this some sort of psychic phenomenon destined for every girl out in the world? It's okay for the "good girls" with the "good dads," but what about the rest of us? The boys' dad left for Los Angeles last year and is not coming back. He has detached himself from any sort of responsibility in taking care of us. I am used to that, but I worry for the boys. They are so sweet and innocent and easy to love. They don't deserve this. I wish I could talk to you, Dad, and you could talk to me in a normal conversation. I know you may not be able to understand me between your sporadic thoughts of buying $50 worth of Ramen Noodles and reciting all the colleges that the past first ladies attended. Do you still have aluminum foil strips hanging from your ceilings to block the waves? I remember three Christmases ago when I told you how concerned I was that my husband didn't have a job and that I was really struggling to support the family. You smiled and said, " He's smart but you know the really smart ones will get the system to pay them not to work." At first I went home and cried thinking you may have faked the whole thing all these years. Now I am smiling realizing that faking a mental illness would qualify you as being mentally ill.

The doctors and the psychiatrists tell me that schizophrenics can live a normal life under medication. I don't think so, and I don't care what they try to tell me. I just want, no I need a daddy that understands me enough to hold and love me and tell me that everything will be all right.

Well, Father's Day is coming soon, and every year it gets harder to find you a card, and now I will have to find one for the boys to send their dad. Do you still throw away your clothes after they get dirty? Instead of going to the Goodwill, I will send you a box of t-shirts. Maybe I'll throw in a bag of cheese puffs, too.

Remembering Daddy

Melissa Mankin
Eagleville School, Grade 5

I remember his black wavy hair perfectly placed upon his head.

I remember afternoon naps lying securely upon his chest.

I remember the strength I felt when he embraced my hand as though I could achieve any feat that came my way.

I remember the endless afternoons of practicing ball in the back yard until I would do things as he thought I should.

I remember the "LOOK" he gave, no words would he say, whenever I misbehaved.

I remember how he would always attend every ballgame, school activity, or church program I was in.

I remember the time he sent flowers on Valentine's Day to help mend my broken heart and let me know things would be okay.

I remember how he made each holiday special through his love for tradition. Whether it was fireworks on the 4th of July, making cranberry sauce for Thanksgiving dinner, or his excitement while hanging stockings awaiting Santa's visit on Christmas morning.

I remember how proud he was when I graduated college.

I remember on my wedding day how he cried as he nervously gave me away and replied, "Her mother and I," when asked who gives this woman to be wed.

I remember the joy he felt as he held my daughters for the first time.

I remember our final words to each other. "I love you," I said. "I love you too," he replied as the Lord took him away on that dark and mournful August day.

I Remember You, Grandmama

Kim Cing
Siegel High School, Grades 9 and 10

I remember those early summer dawns, the heavy, wet heat already rising from the dew on the grass. You would be waiting behind the screen door, reminding me to wipe my sandaled feet.

I remember the lazy mornings. You would be in your recliner crocheting your colorful pillow covers and afghans. Yarn chains, then loop it together, now start your stitches, and make a granny square. "Don't hold it so tight, doll-baby." You patiently taught me how to do it. It's one of the many legacies you left behind.

I remember Granddaddy in his own recliner, grumbling at the characters in his soap operas, the sweet-smelling smoke from his tobacco pipe forming a halo around his head. You would just laugh at him for carrying on so, and your teasing would make him even more belligerent. What a sight the two of you were!

I remember your lunches, usually left-overs from Sunday dinner. You always made enough on Sunday to last all week! Fried chicken, roast and potatoes, chicken and dumplins, fried okra, turnip greens (which I refused to touch), fresh green beans and white corn from the garden, and my favorite . . . macaroni and cheese. It was homemade – big noodles with whole slices of Kraft cheese melted on top. And for dessert, steaming peach cobbler or fried peach pies from the peach tree out back.

I remember busy afternoons outdoors. You would water your plants and flowers or just rock in the chair in the carport. I, on the other hand, would be running around the sprawling yard making up adventures to act out, the pleasant smell of fresh-cut grass filling my nose as Granddaddy went round and round on his Snapper in his overalls.

I remember you encouraged me to make mud pies and climb trees. You even gave me little pans in which to "bake" my pies in the hot summer sun. In the autumn, Troy and I would rake up huge piles of leaves and climb the tree to jump in them. Didn't you worry that we'd break arms and legs? You would get so aggravated because those dry, brittle leaves were so difficult to get out of my long, brown hair. But you were still so careful with the brush while struggling with the unruly mass.

I remember my tire swing in the towering tree beside the driveway. (You know, that tree seems to have shrunk.) Daddy rigged the swing up for us. If we swung out too far and weren't careful, we'd come right back and hit the tree. I don't know how many scrapes I got from the biting bark of that monster!

I remember all the fruits and garden vegetables you tended so gently. You showed me how to choose the ripest tomatoes, how to shuck corn. The strawberry patch was in the back corner. I would sneak as many into my mouth as into the basket. But I guess you knew that all along. You never scolded me for it. When Mama would come to get me, you and Granddaddy and I would be sitting in the carport, in those chairs whose webbing was always breaking. We would all be shelling peas or snapping beans – out of the bucket, SNAP, SNAP, into the bowl.

I remember the rainy days when I moped around inside. You would pull out picture albums, puzzles, and coloring books. You would play with me and my "doll babies," sewing little clothes on your Singer. That red baby carriage was so old and patched up with electric tape. I would play dress up in the back room with the clothes in that metal wardrobe. I loved to find your old hats with the delicate nets that went over my face. You let me play with everything in there and you told me the stories of when you wore those same clothes.

I remember vaguely when Granddaddy passed away. I don't know why it's not very clear in my memory. Maybe my mind just prefers to dwell on the way he was: a devout Christian, a church song leader and deacon, a hard worker. I don't remember you crying much. We were worried about how you would handle living alone. But then again, you always *were* very strong.

I remember when you got sick, the cancer attacking your body. I had never seen you weak before and it was frightening. But like your true self, you fought and prayed, and by God's grace, you won! But not for long . . . it came back and that time it was just too much for your frail body.

I remember coming to see you at the nursing home. You always had a smile for me. Looking back, I wonder how many of those smiles were covering your pain.

I remember you, Grandmama. I wish I had had more time to learn all the lessons you had to teach.

Road Kill

Brian Davis
Oakland High School, Grade 9

It's been said that you always hurt the one you love, but when I was in 7th grade, my dad and I killed my grandpa for Christmas. There was no pre-meditation; we gained nothing. There was no malice involved, no ill-gotten legacy of land or even money stuffed in a mattress. Nor was it a case of Piedmont anger gone terribly awry, what people from those parts once referred to as a "killin'," manslaughter elsewhere but a semi-legal defense in the eyes of many in an area where referring to a millworker as a "linthead" often resulted in one.

But now it's time to fess up. My dad is gone now too, and besides, I was only a barely conscious, hardly willing accomplice. Thirteen year olds weren't tried as adults in 1971, and I'm sure that whatever statute of limitations there is for Accessory to Grandpatricide has long since expired. I am immune from prosecution, and not even sleuths from CSI armed with microscopes and mito-chondrial DNA could convict me today. No other witnesses exist to corroborate my testimony, and the only tangible evidence was eaten by the victim. We killed PawPaw with a possum.

It started innocently enough a week before Christmas. Dad and I had been doing errands until dusk, and we were in work clothes as we were driving home towards the last ray of light on what would become a dark, moonless night. I was engaged in some kind of reverie when our Plymouth Fury, a stolid, tank-like ton and a half mating of Rustbelt excess, locked down, inertia launching my seatbeltless body into the dash when that word meant something-a Gibraltar of unpadded stamped metal fully capable of dashing in the skull of any unfortunate impacting it. The jolt interrupted my reverie with an ascending helix of consciousness and hypnagogia made no clearer by my father's assertion that "I just saw your grandpa's Christmas present."

We were, even by the standards of where I grew up, in the middle of nowhere. I had no idea of what my dad was talking about, and before I could figure anything out, he had abandoned me and the car in the middle of the road and taken off across the yard of the only house for a half mile-this in an area where the only thing taken more seriously than the Third Commandment was the Second Amendment. In short, it was a yard I wouldn't have crossed at gunpoint-a distinct possibility..

Dad receded into the gloaming, and I observed his apparition plant his foot, kick at what appeared to be nothing, and reappear with a satisfied look on his face and a cataleptic critter grasped by its prehensile tail. It was the possum, Didelphis Virginia, a hundred million years of evolutionary stasis that had survived both the dinosaur and automobile, but not my dad. Having recently been in a semi-conscious state, myself,I empathized with the ill-fated marsupial

160

and was stunned when I was instructed to get a gunny sack out of the trunk for us to put him in. I knew my grandpa loved possum-he would eat anything-but there remains no shortage of them in the forty miles that separated our homes, and I remain amazed that one might be considered a gift.

The next day we went to my grandparents bearing the Yuletide bounty, though we did bear one gift we didn't gaily wrap and place under the tree. My grandfather seemed genuinely touched by the gift, for he had a week to prepare it for Christmas. He was a possum gourmand; what Julia Child is to foie gras, he was to the possum. We consigned him to Death Row, a pen in the back of the house, and while the possum got no candlelight vigils or marches of protesters bearing placards asking "What would Pogo do?," the condemned did get more than bread and water. He received cornbread and buttermilk, apparently in copious amounts, for when we returned Christmas Eve, what was once a mere potential road pizza now appeared to be a toothy soccer ball with a hairless tail. A possum is a creature that even the expression "a face that only a mother could love" does not extend to. But that did nothing to prepare me for the spectacle that awaited us at Christmas dinner. We had the usual entrees-- ham, chicken and dumplings, even rabbit, but there, a raft of gristle adrift in a sea of grease, was the piece de resistance, dark, twisted sinewy scraps of something vaguely animal, and as oldest grandchild, I was given first dibs. Diplomacy is not my strong suit, and yet I danced a captivating verbal pas de deux in deference to my elders, all of whom also politely demurred, leaving the entire possum to the paterfamilias-an honor he accepted with gustatory glee. My last memory of that day is our leaving, and I still remember his multiple thanks for his gift.

It was the last time I saw him. New Year's Morning, while tying his shoes, he dropped dead in his living room. The rest of the family has always assumed it was the three packs a day of unfiltered Camels he inhaled, and there was a curious symmetry; it was the last day that cigarette ads were allowed on TV, but Dad and I always knew. It was the possum, the gift that stopped one living.

Christmas

April Holland
Buchananan Elementary School, Kindergarten

A time to…
>Celebrate
>For family and friends
>To eat lots of food
>See lights with no end
>Hang mistletoe
>For playing in the snow

A time to glorify the most precious gift of the Son who was born long ago.